FEROCIOUS,

He'd taken barely half a dozen steps when a raw orange light flared in the darkness among the tents. Screams of pain and terror rose along with the light. He stopped dead, his eyes telling him what was there but his mind refusing to register the message.

A dragon towered among the tents, a dragon that might have escaped from a child's imagination. A fanged and scaled head rose on a long neck, with great yellow eyes glaring out on either side of the long snout. From that snout orange flame roared, like the jet from a flamethrower. He smelled the raw, wrenching foulness of methane and gagged as the dragon belched flame again.

The neck of the monster swept down into a massive body supported on four claw-footed legs. He caught sight of a soldier writhing under one of those feet, blood oozing from him as the dragon's weight slowly crushed him into the ground. Behind the body a long tail stretched off into the darkness and on either side of the body spread immense wings. One of those wings lashed forward into the faces of half a dozen soldiers. Four of the men went down in agony. Two ran, flames streaming from their hair and clothing. They did not get far. Out of the darkness another dragon came sweeping down to land almost in front of them. Then the great scaled head dipped and the fanged jaws closed—on one of them . . .

The Blade Series:

#1 THE BRONZE AXE
#2 THE JADE WARRIOR
#3 JEWEL OF THARN
#4 SLAVE OF SARMA
#5 LIBERATOR OF JEDD
#6 MONSTER OF THE MAZE
#7 PEARL OF PATMOS
#8 UNDYING WORLD
#9 KINGDOM OF ROYTH
#10 ICE DRAGON
#11 DIMENSION OF DREAMS
#12 KING OF ZUNGA
#13 THE GOLDEN STEED
#14 THE TEMPLES OF AYOCAN
#15 THE TOWERS OF MELNON
#16 THE CRYSTAL SEAS
#17 THE MOUNTAINS OF BREGA
#18 WARLORDS OF GAIKON
#19 LOOTERS OF THARN
#20 GUARDIANS OF THE CORAL THRONE
#21 CHAMPION OF THE GODS
#22 THE FORESTS OF GLEOR
#23 EMPIRE OF BLOOD
#24 THE DRAGONS OF ENGLOR

HEROIC FANTASY SERIES 24

RICHARD BLADE

THE DRAGONS OF ENGLOR

by Jeffrey Lord

PINNACLE BOOKS LOS ANGELES

This is a work of fiction. All the characters and events portrayed in this book are fictional, and any resemblance to real people or incidents is purely coincidental.

BLADE #24: THE DRAGONS OF ENGLOR

An original Pinnacle Books edition, published for the first time anywhere.

ISBN: 0-523-40260-0

Produced by Lyle Kenyon Engel

First printing, May 1977
Second printing, October 1977
Third printing, April 1978

Cover illustration by Ken Kelly

Printed in the United States of America

PINNACLE BOOKS, INC.
2029 Century Park East
Los Angeles, California 90067

The Dragons of Englor

Chapter 1

Two tall men walked along a corridor two hundred feet below the Tower of London. Their footsteps raised echoes from the tiled floors and painted cement of the walls.

The man on the right was known only as J. A casual look at him would have suggested that he was a senior civil servant, nearing retirement age after many years of faithful and unobtrusive service. The Oxford accent, the erect carriage, and the flawless, understated tailoring of his dark gray suit all reinforced the impression.

The man on the left was named Richard Blade. He had always been harder to classify than J, and always would be. A dark man, one might have called him—dark hair, dark, closely trimmed beard, skin tanned almost to swarthiness. A wealthy man—he wore a custom-tailored suit, handmade brown shoes, a fine digital watch. A powerful man—under that suit was obviously an athlete's body, massively muscled and conditioned. If asked to guess about Richard Blade, the onlooker would have probably said, "A well-off amateur athlete and man about town."

The onlooker would have been spectacularly wrong about both J and Richard Blade.

J had indeed served the British Crown faithfully and unobtrusively for many years. In espionage a man has to be faithful, and a man who isn't unobtrusive doesn't live very long. J was one of the century's great spymasters and head of the secret intelligence agency MI6. He had also reached an age where a normal man would have been at least thinking about retirement. But those who make distinguished careers in the dim shadowy world of espionage are seldom so normal.

Richard Blade was indeed a trained athlete, and not at all short of money. He'd been one of MI6's finest and deadliest field agents, picked by J himself when fresh out of Oxford. There was nothing of the amateur about him, and there never would be. He was a brilliant and formidable professional in a game more demanding and far deadlier than polo or tennis or steeplechasing.

He was also unique in the whole world. He was the only living human being who could travel into other Dimensions and return safely. It was because of Blade's uniqueness that he and J were walking along the echoing corridor far below the Tower of London. At the end of the corridor lay a series of rooms, and in the last of those rooms stood an enormous computer. That computer was the creation of Lord Leighton, who had the most brilliant mind and usually the worst temper among all of Britian's scientists. Richard Blade's brain would be linked to that computer, so that they formed a single circuit. Then Lord Leighton would pull a red master switch, activating that circuit, and Richard Blade would whirl off into—somewhere else. .

They called that "somewhere else" Dimension X. When the great computer had finished twisting Blade's brain and senses, he saw and smelled somewhere else, heard and felt somewhere else, fought and moved somewhere else. Somehow he always survived and came back alive, sane, and reasonably healthy, to tell of what he had done and seen in the unknown. He was the only living person who could do that, in spite of all the efforts made to find others.

There was much more to what had now become Project Dimension X than simply giving Richard Blade a chance for one incredible adventure after another. Out there in Dimension X lay vast resources of all the things that Britain so desperately needed—land, metals, knowledge. Blade had gone out twenty-three times and come back twenty-three times, but he'd never been able to bring back more than tantalizing samples or hints of the wealth of Dimension X. In spite of all the money, work, thought, and good intentions that had gone into it, the Project still seemed to be doing very little except giving Blade those exotic adventures.

This was becoming a problem, one that would rapidly get worse if things didn't change soon. It was this problem that Blade and J were discussing as they walked down the corridor.

"The total value of what you've brought back in gold and jewels and the like is adding up quite admirably," said J. "The grand total is now over three million pounds."

"That's not enough to cover the whole cost of the Project, is it?" asked Blade. He knew that he should take more interest in the budgetary and administrative side of the Project. He had never been an office type though, or able to concern himself very much with even the most essential paperwork details.

"No. The total investment in the Project since we started is about eleven million. But what you've brought back has helped keep us within what the Prime Minister's Special Fund can absorb."

"I imagine the Prime Minister is happy about that."

"Not happy," said J. "Not at the moment. He's reasonably satisfied with the financial end of the affair, and otherwise—well Leighton's submitted another report."

"And put his foot in it again?" The scientist had a long-standing habit of conceiving and proposing large additions to the Project and its budget at the drop of a hat, without bothering in the least about minor details of trained manpower or financing.

"If you mean, has Lord Leighton made some new and expensive proposals in his report—yes, he has. This time he's sat down and drawn up a comprehensive scheme for the Project for the next three years, covering long-lead time purchases, contingency planning, everything. I hadn't imagined that he had such a grasp of planning techniques."

J sounded genuinely impressed, rather than exasperated as he usually was by Lord Leighton's proposals. "You sound as though you're supporting him sir," said Blade.

"I am," said J. "Or at least I would be, if it would do any good. Leighton's done a fine job. He hasn't asked for anything we shouldn't have had years ago."

Blade hesitated, then fired the decisive question. "How much will it all cost?"

"Four million."

Blade grimaced. "I don't imagine we have much chance of getting that."

"None whatever. It can't possibly come out of the Special Fund, and as for getting a regular appropriation—well, you know as well as I do what the chances are of that, even if it were safe."

Blade nodded silently. The Prime Minister's Special Fund was the only source of money for the Project where no questions would be asked. In Parliament there always had been and always would be those who would question an unidentified expense of five pounds if they thought it would score them political points. With four million pounds they would have a field day, and the security of Project Dimension X would never survive.

It had to survive, though. No other nation knew the secret of inter-Dimensional travel. No other nation appeared to even know that the British had discovered it. Things had to stay this way as long as possible. What the Russians might do if they could tap the secrets of Dimension X was something to give the calmest of men nightmares.

"Besides," J went on, "Parliament wouldn't be inclined to come up with four million pounds for *any* scientific project these days, unless it's got some obvious value." Frustration and a strained temper sounded in J's voice as he continued. "Meanwhile, everybody's moving on ahead of us in a dozen fields. Atomic power—the French are putting breeder reactors into service. Electronics—the Japanese have made half a dozen breakthroughs in superconductors. Genetics—in genetics, we've had reports that the Russians are on the point of cracking the codes for direct genetic manipulation."

"I thought that had already been done," said Blade.

"With bacteria, yes. But this report mentioned work with higher animals, at least up to the level of fish. Of course the results will come more slowly with larger, slower-breeding animals—until they get cloning perfected. So we may not have to worry for a few years. But—imagine a swarm of mutated and cloned sharks let loose as a terror weapon, or to form a submarine detection network?"

Blade nodded. Anybody with a little scientific knowledge and a good imagination could in a very short time conjure up a dozen horrible results of direct genetic manipulation. It had been pure science fiction for a number of years. Now it was looming closer and closer as an unpleasant reality.

"Of course this makes matters even worse for us. *Every* scientist is trying to clutch Parliament by the lapels and shake an appropriation out of it for his particular project. If by some miracle we did get our four million, we'd have two-thirds of the research establishment howling for our blood. Even Leighton can't do his best without more cooperation than we'd get under those circumstances."

"So where exactly do you feel that we stand, sir?" asked Blade. They were approaching the door into the computer rooms themselves. He wanted to get the conversation done and J calmed down before they entered. He had never seen J so close to losing his patience with anything or anybody, with the occasional exception of Lord Leighton.

J seemed to realize how much his agitation was boiling over. He took a deep breath and his posture became even more erect.

"What we need is for you to bring back something extraordinary from Dimension X. It could be a scientific breakthrough whose value would be obvious even to the most idiotic backwoods back-bencher who's forgotten the small amount of physics and mathematics he ever learned. If it were that obviously valuable, we'd be able to get our four million with no questions asked. We would simply call ourselves a "secret research facility" that had produced this discovery, and ask politely if they wanted us to produce some more like it."

Blade laughed. "Yes. Under those circumstances we might wind up with more money than we could spend."

J fixed the younger man with a look of mock severity. "Richard, that shows how little you know of administration. There is no such sum at the moment. Nor do I expect that either of us will live long enough to see the day when there is."

"No doubt," said Blade. "What is the second thing I could bring back to help the Project out of its hole?"

"A new process or product—something we could sell to private industry for at least—well, for whatever the market would bear. I wish I could be more optimistic about the chances of that."

Blade nodded. He'd brought back a good many products and processes decades or centuries beyond anything known in Home Dimension. Unfortunately no one had yet been able to duplicate any of them on any useful scale. What the devil! The scientists were still struggling to duplicate teksin, and he'd brought the sample of that superplastic back from his first trip to Tharn, longer ago than he cared to think about.

Now they were at the entrance to the computer rooms. The door slid open in front of them. They moved on, through the familiar sequence of rooms crammed to the ceiling with supporting equipment and the technicians to handle it. They came to the door of the main computer room, waited while electronic monitoring systems scanned them and opened the door, then entered.

Lord Leighton's voice floated down to them from high above. "Richard, you can go ahead and change. Everything's in order. I'm just taking the chance to make a routine inspection." The sound of metal tapping on metal followed before Blade could say a word in reply. The scientist was back at work, and he quite thoroughly detested making polite conversation at such times.

Blade didn't blame him. In fact, it was surprising that Leighton had bothered to speak at all. The scientist was more than eighty years old, his spine twisted by a hunched back, his legs almost as twisted by polio. Yet there he was, clambering about somewhere high above, putting himself to inconvenience and strain to make an inspection that a technician a third his age could have done easily. Lord Leighton was a man who considered any job half-done unless and until he had done it or at least checked it himself.

Blade only hoped that he could remain half as conscientious and dedicated when age and physical frailty caught up with him.

Blade followed his usual path around the gray, crackle-finished bulks of the computer's consoles, to the changing room carved out of the rock wall. By now he could have followed that path blindfolded or in pitch darkness, without missing a turn or a step.

He could also have gone through the routine in the room in his sleep, he had done it so often. So he made a special effort to be alert during every moment of the routine. Long experience had taught him that the minute you start writing something off as "routine," you start making careless mistakes. Blade didn't want to run any risk of that with any part of a trip into Dimension X. They still knew just enough about the process to know how much more they had to learn, and how many things could go wrong.

So he was as careful now as he had ever been, as he stripped to the skin and smeared himself from head to toe with greasy black cream. It felt dreadful and smelled worse, but it was intended to prevent burns from the massive jolt of electricity passing through his body in the moment of transition.

He took a loincloth down from a peg on the wall and tied it on. He always wore one, although none of them had ever passed into Dimension X with him. He had carried a gold ring on one trip and his old commando knife on another. Both of these had made the round trip with him, and both were now under intensive examination to reveal what special qualities they had.

Meanwhile, there was nothing else he could find that he'd had for many years and would also be useful in Dimension X. There were plenty of things he could take that he hadn't owned for years, but would any of them make the trip? Almost certainly not, from past experience. They would just add more uncertainties where there were already too many. It would be safer to go off into Dimension X, prepared to arrive with nothing but his wits and his naked body. He'd survived that way often enough before.

Blade finished knotting the loincloth, stepped out of the room, and walked to the glass booth that stood in the very center of the room. He sat down in the metal chair inside the booth, feeling the rubber of the seat and back cold against his bare skin, and settled down to relaxing as much as he could. He always succeeded, although he could never completely keep his mind off what might be waiting for him in Dimension X.

Meanwhile Lord Leighton practically ran in circles around the chair, pulling wires in a dozen different colors out of odd parts of the computer. Each wire ended in a gleaming metal electrode, shaped like the head of a cobra. Lord Leighton taped each electrode to Blade's skin. Then he stepped back, briefly surveyed his work with a satisfied smile, and walked across the room to the main control panel.

The panel was already lit up like a psychedelic Christmas tree. The computer's program was running on the main sequence, running steadily toward the moment when it would be ready to hurl Richard Blade away on his next journey.

In these last moments Blade always felt very much at peace with the world. He also knew better than ever how simple his job in the Project really was. No research to do, no appropriations to fight for, no security problems to track down and handle. At the moment, J was still fighting to sidetrack Scotland Yard from its search for the "mystery hero" who'd vanished after saving a dozen lives in a train wreck a few months ago. That mystery hero was Blade, who'd vanished to avoid publicity that would endanger the Project, then gone off into Dimension X while J was left holding the sack.

Before Blade's mind could form another thought, Lord Leighton's hand descended smoothly onto the red master switch and drew it even more smoothly down to the bottom of its slot.

The floor beneath the booth dropped away into a swirling black nothingness. The booth and Blade inside it seemed to hang suspended above the blackness, with the room and the computer consoles and Leighton and J still clearly visible all around.

Then the blackness began to turn red and come alive with dark fumes that swirled around Blade without burning or choking or even brushing against him. They seemed to swirl right through him, for suddenly he was as intangible as they were.

Beneath the redness a fiery yellow began to glow, rising up through the redness, rising up through the fumes, pouring a fierce light over the computer and the men. They seemed to dissolve in that light, as if they'd been dropped into boiling acid.

The light grew brighter, and Blade saw that the booth was gone from around the chair, and then the chair was gone from under him. He was alone, seated on nothingness in the middle of raw yellow fire that should have burned but did not.

He was still alone when the yellow fire faded slowly away into blackness and the blackness swallowed him up and blanked out all his senses.

Chapter 2

Richard Blade awoke slowly, with his head throbbing as usual. The sun was out—he could feel it on his skin. So he lay quietly on his back, his eyes closed against the light, while the headache faded and all his other senses built up a picture of the world around him.

There was the sun. There was a definite breeze, warm but with a sort of faint undertone of damp coolness. It felt very much like the breeze on an English spring day. There were bushes around him and trees overhead, their leaves rustling in the breeze. There were flowers blooming close enough for their scents to reach Blade. He recognized roses and half a dozen others, all surprisingly familiar. Under him, prickling gently against his bare skin, was short, thick grass, still slightly damp from a night's dew. It felt trimmed as close and as neatly as any lawn or park.

He could hear the faint drone of insects, the fainter chirps of birds, far away and fainter still the barking of a dog. Still farther away was a subdued murmuring and muttering. If Blade had been in England, he would have called it heavy traffic on a road several miles away.

The headache was fading now. Blade sat up, shaded his eyes to keep from getting the full blast of the sun, and opened them.

He was between two rows of bushes, with trees arching overhead to form almost a canopy. Through that canopy he could see cotton-puff clouds ambling across a deep blue and faintly hazy sky. On a branch seemingly close enough to touch, a bird perched. It was the size and shape of an English robin, except that its breast was a genuine crimson rather than a reddish orange. As he watched, it sprang into the air. He noticed that its outspread wings had pale, almost whitish tips.

The grass under him was definitely a lawn—recently mowed, too. He picked up a handful of clippings and let them sift through his fingers and scatter on the breeze. The ground under the bushes was freshly weeded, too. This was obviously a park or some rather extensive and well-kept estate.

That suggested a fairly respectable civilization. Blade was pleased. He could survive anywhere, among any kind of people. He had done so many times in the past, and no doubt would do so many times in the future, until either his luck ran out for good or until someone else was chosen to go off into Dimension X. Yet he was still a good deal more comfortable among people who took baths, wrote and read books, and were not in the habit of killing strangers on sight.

Blade stood up and started walking along the strip of grass between the two rows of bushes. He would do well to get out of this park or estate and get to some place where he could find some clothes. After that it would be safe to start exploring and trying to meet people. Civilized Dimensions had at least one disadvantage. They had proper authorities, and those proper authorities often disapproved of people wandering around dressed as Blade was, in nothing at all.

Blade quickly saw that a fence ran across the far end of the grass strip, completely blocking his exit. He moved on, noticing that the well-trimmed bushes on either side of him looked remarkably like an English privet hedge, although the berries were pale blue rather than grayish white.

Blade came up to the fence. It was a plain undecorated piece of work, wrought iron painted flat black. Peering around the hedges, he could see the fence stretching away in either direction. It looked like a hundred other fences he had seen in similar parks and estates in Home Dimension. Nothing surprising or unusual about it at all.

On the other side of the fence was a white gravel path, neatly raked and weeded, also stretching off in either direction as far as Blade could see. He could see quite a distance, and all he could see appeared to be more park, more trees, more pruned bushes, flowerbeds, and neatly mowed lawns. Very far away he thought he could make out an occasional quick-moving splash of color and hear the murmur that sounded like traffic noises.

On the other side of the path was something just as familiar as all the rest. In fact, it was so familiar that Blade began to find it vaguely disturbing. It was a white porcelain drinking fountain with brass fittings, mounted on a plain concrete base. It was thoroughly twentieth century British, except that this wasn't twentieth century Britain.

Or was it? Blade found a thought slowly forming in his mind. It was not vague at all, but it was even more disturbing than the drinking fountain.

Was he still in Home Dimension, even in England? Had the computer finally misfired, merely shifting him a few miles sideways in space and perhaps a few months forward or backward in time? Was he in a park in the suburbs of London, and were those distant murmurings that sounded like traffic noises exactly that?

It was too soon to call that *the* explanation. There was that robin that wasn't quite a robin, that privet hedge that wasn't quite a privet. Also, there was no sound of air traffic overhead, neither jets nor light planes nor helicopters.

True, all of this. But Blade had to admit that birds and shrubs weren't things he knew very well. Both the "robin" and the "privet" could be something perfectly common and respectable that he simply didn't recognize. As for the air traffic—well, there were undoubtedly parks even in the suburbs of London a good distance from any air traffic lanes. The same thing would be even truer of other towns and cities in southern England.

On the whole, Blade rather hoped that he wasn't still in England. The public authorities there definitely frowned on people wandering around naked in public. Unless he was very lucky in the matter of finding clothes, he would be arrested sooner or later. Then there would have to be identifications and explanations made, somehow, preferably without involving J or anybody else even remotely connected with the Project. A hundred different things could go wrong, possibly reviving the whole "mystery hero" problem or even breaching the security of Project Dimension X.

There were no spikes on top of the fence. Blade put both hands on the upper crossbar and got ready to swing himself over it. He wanted to inspect that drinking fountain, and, if it was as authentic as it looked, get a drink of water from it. Then he would be on his way. The park seemed fairly deserted—it was probably a weekday. But somebody was bound to wander by sooner or later.

Blade had just taken a firm grip when he heard a weirdly familiar sound overhead, growing rapidly louder. His head jerked up, in time for him to see a large four-engined transport plane sail low overhead. He got a good look at it as it passed barely a thousand feet above him. Long after it was out of sight and hearing, his mind tried furiously to sort out what he'd seen.

Unmistakably, the plane was a Royal Air Force Lockheed C-130 Hercules, with four turboprops. It was identical to those he'd seen at RAF bases and even parachuted from a few times. It was identical from nose to tail, including the form of the insignia on the wings, the camouflage pattern, and the lettering of the serial numbers. If it had been a little lower, Blade suspected he'd have been able to identify the squadron badge on the nose.

He was still in England. Suddenly it was hard to believe anything else. It was more than hard, it was almost impossible. He could certainly not find plausible the idea of a Dimension X that flew airplanes virtually identical to those of Home Dimension.

No, he was still in England. The computer had slipped up and there was an end to it. Blade shrugged. There were going to be all sorts of problems, unless by some chance he was lucky enough to escape arrest and get to clothes, money, and a telephone. If he was that lucky, a quick call to the Project's secret number would raise J, and he and the older man could be dining at J's club tonight. That would certainly set the all-time record for a quick trip through the computer!

Blade felt like laughing with one breath and swearing with the next. It was ludicrous. Here he was, after all the ordeal of another brain-twisting by the computer, still in England. Here he was, in no danger of either being hailed as a god or sacrificed to one, in no real danger of anything except insect bites and arrest for indecent exposure!

It was also unpleasant to think about what it might mean if the computer had developed a new quirk. But that was a worry for the future, and in any case more for Lord Leighton than for him. Here and now, it was time to get moving in search of those clothes, some money, and a telephone, and to put an end to this nonsense.

In the next moment Blade realized he should have got moving a little sooner. Brisk footsteps sounded on the path to the left. He sprang back from the fence, looking around for a hiding place.

Before he could find any, two people strode swiftly into view, a man and a woman. The man was tall and large-framed, with an erect bearing and a commanding air about him. His hair and large mustache were thick and gray, and his face was red but showed no softness or sagging. He wore British Army battledress and a black beret. Blade could not make out his regimental badges or his rank. The battledress suggested a senior NCO—British Army officers seldom wore it off-duty. But the man's manner suggested a field-grade officer—a senior lieutenant colonel, perhaps, who'd kept himself in first-class physical condition.

The woman looked like the perfect wife for such a man. She was only an inch or two shorter than he was, with large capable-looking hands and a long, almost horsey face. She wore a long-sleeved blouse and a gray tweed skirt down to mid-calf, and carried a sweater over one arm.

As the couple came into view, the woman started to unfold the sweater from her arm. As she did, her eyes swung toward the side of the path and fell squarely on a Richard Blade who would in that moment have cheerfully paid any price to become invisible.

The woman's eyes and mouth opened wide. For a moment Blade thought she was going to faint or scream hysterically. Instead she whirled, grabbed her husband's arm, and pointed with the other hand. "Michael—there's a drunken man in the bushes!"

The man whirled to look where his wife was pointing. His own eyes widened, then his hand made a dive for his belt. For the first time Blade noticed that the man was wearing a holstered sidearm on his belt. His large hand moved with surprising speed and came up holding a businesslike black automatic.

"What the devil—!" the man snapped out, in unmistakably plain English with an educated accent. Then:

"Halt!"

—as Blade whirled and took to his heels. A second "Halt!" rang out behind him as he sprinted back the way he'd come. He was busy looking for a break in the bushes, where he could get out of the officer's sight. There was no point in trying to hide now, not in this park. The hunt would be on soon enough, and his best chance of avoiding it would be to get as far away as possible as fast as possible.

Blade ran on. At every step he half expected to hear the automatic crack and to hear a bullet whistle past him—or feel it drive into his body.

A low place in the bushes appeared to his right. He swerved without slowing and leaped without breaking his stride. He soared high, landed on his feet on the other side, and kept right on going. He could hear the officer blowing loudly and shrilly on a whistle. He did not slow down until the sound of the whistle faded away behind him. Then he started off more slowly, in a direction the sun told him was west. Now he moved carefully from one piece of cover to another, with long-practiced skill.

Blade could practically do this sort of movement in his sleep. So now he could spare some thought for the little brush with the military man. There'd been something distinctly and disturbingly odd about it. A British Army officer or NCO might conceivably wear battledress off-duty. But he would never carry a sidearm while strolling through a public park with his wife.

Never, that is, except in wartime.

Blade frowned. Could he have been pushed a few years into the future, into a time when Britain was somehow at war again? Perhaps. It seemed unlikely, though. A war large enough to have army officers wandering around with their sidearms would almost certainly have produced many other changes, changes he would have seen already. He remembered the books he'd read and the pictures he'd seen of World War II. A park like this would have had the fences torn down for their metal, posters plastered all over, and perhaps an anti-aircraft gun or two lurking in the bushes.

It was unlikely but not impossible. After all he'd seen and experienced in Dimension X, "impossible" was a word Richard Blade refused to use.

If he'd traveled forward in time, even only a few years, it was all the more necessary to avoid arrest until he'd sorted things out a bit more. In a Britain at war, never mind where, why, or with whom, the authorities would be more than usually suspicious about unidentified and unidentifiable people found wandering naked in the public parks. It might take weeks instead of days before he could make a phone call to anybody who could vouch for him.

But *would* there be anyone who could vouch for him? Both J and Lord Leighton were old men who might well be dead by now. Then what? There would doubtless be people who remembered him still working in Intelligence. There wouldn't be anyone cleared to know about the Project, though—assuming it was still in existence. That would complicate explaining how he came to be where he was, to put it mildly.

That wasn't the worst of it, either. There were all sorts

of paradoxes that could crop up in time travel, such as meeting another Richard Blade doing useful war work for Intelligence here and now. If that happened, Blade didn't care to think about what else might happen. Confronted with *two* Richard Blades, the authorities might very well decide to lock up the odd Blade out and throw away the key—or possibly even make him quietly disappear some night.

Blade suddenly realized that he might be in a good deal more danger than he'd thought. He would not die of plague or as a sacrifice to the local gods here. But there was still a much better chance than usual that he'd never get back to where he'd started. If the computer had bobbled him forward in time to a Britain at war, it might be the last bobble it ever made with him.

The noises that sounded like traffic, and probably were, grew steadily louder as he moved. After a while he could see a main road off in the distance, through the trees, and a good deal of traffic passing along it. He could not clearly make out the types of vehicles, but they seemed to be mostly trucks of various sizes. Some of them seemed to be painted in military olive drab.

Blade shifted his direction. If possible, he wanted to come out of the park in a quiet neighborhood, not onto a busy road with dozens of people in sight, some of them probably armed and alert.

Two more aircraft flew over the park. One was a jet fighter, moving too fast for Blade to identify the type. The other was a small helicopter. It seemed to be passing rather low overhead, and Blade had an unpleasant moment's wondering if it was looking for him. Then the helicopter moved on and so did Blade.

What lay on the other three sides of this park was a matter of educated guesswork. Blade kept angling steadily farther and farther away from the road, listening to the traffic noises slowly fade. He also listened for any sound that might give him a clue of what lay in the other directions. He was as alert as a hunting animal. He also had to fight an urge to laugh at the notion of having to use his skills in escape, evasion, silent movement, and all the rest here in his native country.

Suddenly the sound of voices came from the other side of a screen of bushes. Blade dropped flat on the ground and listened. He heard footsteps, the metallic *chink* of military equipment, then more voices. One of them had an unmistakable flavor of cockney.

" 'E must've 'eaded this way, or Blooey'd 'ave picked 'im up."

"Don't know 'bout that," said the other voice. "If he's running around starkers, he might be a bit off in the head. I'm not going to worry, no matter what Sergeant Bloody Lamb says."

Blade lay still until both the footsteps and the voices faded away, and for a little longer after that. The hunt was on, that was certain. It sounded as if the army was taking part in it. That made no sense, unless he was in or near some military installation, which didn't seem likely.

In any case, he'd have to turn back, at least for the moment. The bushes and trees ahead made a barrier too thick to push through quickly or quietly. Blade rose to a crouch and began retracing his steps, moving even more quietly than before.

After a hundred yards or so he changed direction again. His new course took him down a gentle slope, heavily overgrown with low shrubs. He was able to keep under cover all the way down the slope, until it suddenly steepened and he found himself standing on the edge of a stream. The stream flowed through a steep-sided gulley nearly eight feet deep. Fifty feet upstream a narrow, whitewashed wooden bridge crossed the gulley.

Crossing the stream looked like a gamble, whichever way he did it. But he didn't seem to have any choice, and he certainly had no time to lose. He carefully scanned every tree and bush and patch of open ground he could see. Then he slipped from the shelter of the last bush and slid down the side of the gulley.

He landed with a faint splash in a slow-moving trickle of cool, muddy water. He crossed it in two steps and began to look for handholds in the bank in front of him. Just one, and he'd be up the bank and back under cover.

Blade was just reaching out for a likely-looking root when someone shouted angrily.

"Hi there! Stop, in the name of the law!"

A large man in a London policeman's uniform was standing on the bridge, glowering down at Blade. He was also pointing at Blade an equally unmistakable and thoroughly vicious-looking submachine gun. It was a remarkably incongruous weapon for a London bobby, normally armed with nothing more formidable than a truncheon and his bare fists.

Blade's eyes flicked quickly up and down the gulley. There was no cover he could possibly reach before the bobby could put half a dozen bullets through him. He stepped away from the bank into the center of the stream, turned to face the bobby, and carefully raised both hands over his head.

The chase was over. It would have been over even if he'd had a weapon to pick off the bobby, submachine gun and all. Security in this wartime Britain must be very tight indeed if even the bobbies were carrying submachine guns. In that case, resisting arrest would be fatal, sooner or later.

"That's *much* better," said the bobby, with grim cheerfulness. "Now, come toward me, *verrrrry* slowly, and just stand quiet where I tell you."

Blade shuffled toward the bridge, the oozy mud of the stream bottom sucking at his feet each time he put them down and clinging to them each time he raised them. It was like walking through a bowl of sticky oatmeal.

Blade was ten feet away when the bobby held up one hand. Blade noticed that he was wearing tan gloves with some sort of red badge on the backs. No doubt a wartime uniform change.

"Right there, now." The bobby took the whistle hanging around his neck, stuck it in his mouth, and began blowing long shrill blasts. The submachine gun remained pointed straight at Blade.

Now that he was close enough, Blade recognized the submachine gun the bobby was carrying. It was an Israeli Uzi. It was an odd weapon to see in the hands of a London bobby, but under the circumstances neither surprising nor sinister. The Uzi was one of the best submachine guns in the world. When the war broke out, no doubt someone in the Ministry of Defense had arranged a license to manufacture it here in Britain. Just another detail of this new and confusing time in which Blade found himself. There was going to be a whole great mass of those details before things got sorted out for him, if they ever did.

The bobby stopped blowing his whistle. "Now, I don't know what you think you're doing, running around without any clothes on. This is Englor, not some black country down in the tropics. We've got laws, and at a time like this—" For a moment the bobby seemed too disgusted over Blade's behavior to go on, but that moment didn't last long. The bobby's lecture did.

As it went on, Blade began to wonder if the man had some sort of speech defect. Every time he spoke the name of the country, it came out "Englor." Something wasn't working right—either the policeman's tongue or Blade's hearing.

Before the bobby could finish reading Blade the whole lecture, help arrived in the form of two soldiers. Both wore battledress and combat webbing and were also carrying Uzis. Hard on their heels appeared the military man Blade had first met, his pistol still in his hand. His face was a good deal redder than before.

"Is this the man, sir?" asked the bobby.

The man stared at Blade. It was a cold and unfriendly stare. Then he nodded and holstered his pistol. "I am Lieutenant Colonel Michael Morris, Duke of Pembroke's Own Light Infantry. Who might you be?"

Blade did a quick set of mental calculations. Refusing to give his name would be extremely suspicious. Giving a false name would be just as bad. What would be a false name under the circumstances? "Richard Blade" might get him in as much hot water as any name he could make up on the spur of the moment. On the other hand, it would stand up better under any interrogation with truth serum or lie detectors, and he had to reckon on that possibility. All in all, it would probably be better to give his own name.

"Richard Blade."

"Well, Mr. Blade," said the colonel. "I don't know what you think you're up to, trotting about the parks in your—in your present state of dress. But I'm quite sure a magistrate will be interested in finding out as soon as possible."

That was no surprise. Blade wondered if the next question from Colonel Morris would be where he'd left his clothes. Blade hoped that question would remain unasked, because it could not be easily answered. At least it could not be answered in any way that would not lead to all sorts of other questions and in the end probably to danger for the secret of Dimension X. Blade was determined to keep that secret, even from his own countrymen and at the cost of his own life. He would only relax on that point if he found himself face to face with J or Lord Leighton, alive and in the flesh.

Apparently Colonel Morris didn't care about Blade's clothes. He merely motioned to one of the soldiers, who threw a folded poncho down to Blade. Blade unfolded it, pulled it over his head, and scrambled up the side of the gulley. Morris took salutes from the two soldiers and the bobby, then strode briskly off down the path. The bobby led Blade off in the opposite direction, with the two soldiers falling in behind. The bobby had slung his submachine gun, but Blade noticed the two soldiers still held theirs at the ready.

The little procession tramped briskly back through the park, retracing more of Blade's steps, heading directly back toward the main road. Blade found himself becoming steadily more alert and observant out of sheer curiosity. What had happened to his country since he'd stepped into the computer, with the passage of time and the strains of this new war? Who was the enemy? Who was winning? He wanted answers to these and a hundred other questions.

In a few more minutes they reached the main road. It stretched away in either direction, bordered on one side by the park and on the other by a mixture of ordinary suburban villas and small shops. Blade looked at some of the signs in the shop windows. Nothing out of the ordinary there, although he didn't recognize some of the brand names. There also seemed to be fewer advertisements for beer, and more for wine. Well, if there was a war on and France was an ally, why not? Nothing surprising there, although he rather hoped that one could still get Mackeson's Stout. It had always been one of his favorite drinks.

To Blade's right was a police van. It was dark blue, with a large crest and some white lettering that he couldn't recognize on the door facing him. The two soldiers swung away to the left. Blade looked after them and saw four large army trucks and two tank transporters parked by the curb. All six vehicles had ring-mounted machine guns on top of the cabs, with soldiers in black berets manning them. Other soldiers were emerging from the park and climbing into the backs of the four trucks.

On each of the two tank transporters sat two small tanks. Like the Uzi submachine guns, they were a perfectly recognizable type. They were Scorpions, the light reconnaissance tanks the British Army had introduced a few years before. Some of the antennas and other external hardware were different, but the silhouettes seemed virtually identical. Blade felt somewhat relieved. He definitely couldn't have been pushed too far into the future if the RAF still flew C-130s and the British Army still used Scorpion tanks.

All this time, traffic had been passing back and forth along the road in front of him. He'd noticed a perfectly ordinary mix of cars and trucks and buses, with an occasional motorcycle or scooter. Now his eyes were drawn to a large green truck that pulled up to the curb in front of a newsstand. Several bundles of newspapers were thrown out and the truck started off again. Another policeman climbed out of the police van, darted across the street in the intervals between cars, and bought an armful of newspapers from the boy at the stand.

Blade's own bobby took his arm firmly and led him toward the van. As they approached, the other man laid most of the newspapers down on the hood of the car, then opened the one he held. Blade looked at the newspaper, and suddenly he felt all his internal organs from his throat down to his groin turn into solid ice.

The newspaper had the exact form of the familiar London *Times*. But it called itself *Imperial Times*. Under the newspaper's name was a motto, "For Emperor, For Englor." Its price was given as "One Imperial Shilling."

That was bad enough, but it wasn't the worst. The headlines read, bold and black:

RUSSLANDER ULTIMATUM. RED FLAMES SAY: EVACUATE NORDSBERGEN. FOREIGN MINISTRY SAYS HOSTILITIES NOW INEVITABLE.

Worst of all was the date. Somehow, this was the same day as it had been when Blade sat down with the computer. The day, the month, and the year were all identical.

Blade shook his head. Either his eyes were telling him more lies than he could imagine, or else he was not in the future.

Yet this wasn't the England of Home Dimension, either. It was a land—an empire—called Englor, facing war with somebody called the Red Flames who ruled a land called Russland.

Where and *when* was he?

Chapter 3

There was a long, painful moment for Blade. He felt utterly alone, as alone and isolated as he had ever felt while passing from Home Dimension into Dimension X. Never in all his life had he felt quite so confused, quite so disoriented, or quite so close to the brink of outright fear.

The moment came to an end as Blade's superbly disciplined mind reasserted its control. Now he could once again ask himself a few basic questions, and this time he could also come up with some sort of answers.

Where was he? Undeniably, in spite of all the signs that pointed the other way, he was in Dimension X. The computer had done its work as well or as badly as ever.

However, this was a Dimension unlike any other he'd ever entered. This Dimension looked and sounded and *felt* so much like the Home Dimension he'd left that it was perfectly possible to mistake the one for the other.

Blade conjured up a mental image of Dimension X as an endless series of different worlds, lined up side by side and stretching out of sight into—call it infinity, for want of a better name. Anyway, in this series a world like Gaikon with its warlords or Brega with its warrior women would be far down the line, far away from Home Dimension. This Dimension where he'd landed, on the other hand, would lie practically next door to Home Dimension.

So far so good. Lord Leighton could undoubtedly find a thousand and one flaws in that image if he had the chance. But Lord Leighton was in the England of Home Dimension and Blade was here in the Englor of Dimension X. The precise accuracy of the image didn't matter. What did matter was that Blade found it useful for settling and arranging his thoughts.

So he was here, in this next-door Dimension that seemed so much like home. "Seemed" was perhaps the most important word in that sentence. The people of this Dimension carried submachine guns and flew airplanes and drove tanks and trucks and cars. They wore the same uniforms and drank the same drinks and probably made love in familiar ways.

Deceptively familiar. That would be the real danger for him in this Dimension—forgetting that it *was* Dimension X, in spite of everything that positively shouted otherwise. Forgetting that one little fact could lead to embarrassing mistakes.

Or worse than embarrassing. That was another problem this Dimension offered, one which Blade had only rarely encountered before. This was an advanced, civilized, organized society, one that was also on the very edge of war.

In more primitive Dimensions, Blade could escape punishment for mistakes by simply hitting the nearest dozen people over the head and taking to his heels. No one could follow him faster than a horse could gallop, and no one could search him out in the wilderness if he didn't want to be found. No one would think his behavior at all unusual, either.

Here in Englor things would be very different. He would have to escape from a dozen men with Uzis, not a dozen with swords or spears. If he did escape, they could pursue him in cars and helicopters and planes, with tear gas and rifles with telescopic sights and infrared detection devices for night work.

If by some chance he did get clear, there would be no wilderness with game and fruit to live on, or wandering tribesmen and hunters to take him in. There would be cities and suburbs, towns and villages, farms no farther than a telephone call from their neighbors. Everywhere there would be hotelkeepers and salsclerks and bus drivers, asking for money or identification or both before they would lift a finger to do anything for him.

Of course, hitting people in the first place simply wouldn't do! Hitting one person would get him locked up. Hitting a dozen would get him locked up for a long time. Killing anybody would be even worse. Blade somehow did not think Englor would be reluctant to impose the death penalty.

Blade was no foolish romantic believer in the virtues of primitive societies. He was very conscious of the advantages of antibiotics, jet planes, hot showers, and guns. At the same time, he was painfully aware that it was a much tougher proposition escaping from civilized captors, if and when escaping became necessary.

There was only one solution, at least for now. He would have to behave himself so that he would not get into any more trouble than he was already, and therefore would have no compelling reason to escape. If the penalty for indecent exposure was fifty pounds or thirty days—well, not having the fifty pounds, he'd serve out the thirty days as a model prisoner and then see what his prospects were when they let him out. His first and foremost goal would be to make sure that they did let him out on time, and everything else would be set aside for the time being.

After he got out, things could be different. Being in an advanced society had its benefits as well as its headaches. Englor was only similar to Britain, not identical. It was quite possible that research and development in some key areas had followed different paths than in Britain. It was almost certain that research and development were more generously financed, at least in those areas useful for military purposes. That was an almost universal rule in any civilized society that faced a major war.

These differences in research and development could mean much or little. They could mean nothing more than slightly improved versions of essentially Home Dimension articles, from jet planes down to bootlaces and emergency rations. They could also mean some fundamental breakthroughs that could easily be translated into hardware—and hard cash—if he could bring the details back to Home Dimension. If he could bring back the secrets of a new and superior missile guidance system, for example—well, generals and admirals would be fighting each other in the halls outside Lord Leighton's office for the privilege of giving money to Project Dimension X!

Blade was so preoccupied sorting out his own thoughts and planning his own best course of action that he forgot completely about the policemen waiting to take him before a magistrate. He was reminded of their existence only when one of them elbowed him sharply in the ribs.

"Wake up there, chum, and climb in. It's time we got moving."

Blade shook himself back into some sort of alertness and climbed into the front seat of the van. He was promptly handcuffed to a bar on the dashboard. Then the other policeman climbed into the back seat, his Uzi still aimed in Blade's general direction. Doors slammed shut, the motor purred to life, and the driver swung the van out into traffic.

Apparently, a simple indecent-exposure case was nothing to cause a great fuss. From the conversation of the two policemen, Blade realized that he'd been a victim of bad luck as much as anything else. The military convoy had been passing by the park when Colonel Morris called the police.

The convoy commander had volunteered his men to help search the park for the naked man, with the idea of giving them a little practical fieldwork. Without the soldiers' help, the police could hardly have covered the park thoroughly enough to catch Blade, Uzis or no Uzis.

The van rolled smoothly through traffic, without the siren wailing or the roof light flashing. Blade had plenty of opportunities to watch London passing—this London that was the capital of the Empire of Englor.

Most of the wines advertised seemed to come from a country called Gallia—no doubt this Dimension's version of France. Blade saw no other countries mentioned anywhere—above all, nothing that might possibly be an equivalent of the United States of America.

This Dimension held the Empire of Englor, where he was now. It held Russland, whose Red Flames were for some reason or other Englor's archenemies. It held Gallia, which made wine, and it held Nordsbergen, which the Red Flames were asking somebody, persumably Englor, to evacuate under threat of war.

Four countries, and that was apparently all. Blade began to wonder if this Dimension was such a close neighbor to Home Dimension as he'd thought. There seemed to be a good deal missing from this world, including about a hundred countries. At least a dozen of them would have been mentioned in any number of advertisements and newspapers easily visible as he passed. Blade had the odd sensation of being in a world created in a startling likeness to Home Dimension, then for some reason left unfinished.

The van was keeping to the main road. From the signs Blade could read its name—"Agar Road S.W." There was no such road that he could recall in Home Dimension London, but there was very little else to remind him that he was not passing through the inner suburbs of his home city. The news vendors, the pubs, the small parks, the railroad station with the crowded orange electric train pulling in—all of these were familiar. The only jarring details were the headlines the news vendors had posted up, and the fact that the electric train had "Imperial Railways" in large blue letters on both sides of all three cars.

A few blocks past the railroad station, the police van turned off Agar Road and began to follow a winding route through an industrial district. Here it was even harder for Blade to remember that he was in Dimension X. The factory buildings were grimy brick and grimier glass, with corrugated iron roofs. High above them rose tall brick chimneys, and around them spread the cracking asphalt of parking lots, the rusty rails of industrial spur lines, and occasional faded and straggling patches of grass that still fought on against fumes and neglect. There was nothing here to tell Blade what city he was in, let alone what Dimension.

Then suddenly the road took them around the corner of a factory, and Blade was abruptly reminded where he was and what he might be facing. In a brick courtyard formed by three large warehouses stood four tracked vehicles, each mounting four launching tubes for guided missiles. One large van appeared to house controls, another appeared to be living quarters. A large radar antenna stood on the roof of each of the warehouses, slowly rotating. Among them, the three antennas covered the complete circle of the horizon. They stood ready to detect any low-flying intruders and feed data to the computers in the van and the missiles ready on their launchers.

The missiles and their supporting equipment didn't match any design Blade had seen or heard of in Home Dimension. That didn't matter. They were obviously not much different from a dozen types in service in Home Dimension.

What did matter was what it meant to see the missiles here. They were a vivid, even harsh reminder that this was a Dimension on the verge of war—and war with modern weapons, with all their monstrous capacity for wholesale destruction.

The police van eventually emerged on the other side of the factory belt and pulled up at a sprawling gray stone police headquarters. Blade was unloaded, led inside, and processed with a calm and methodical efficiency. Apparently the London police ran to the same type of solid professionalism here as they did in Home Dimension.

Business was slow, so Blade spent the night in a cell by himself. The food was no better and no worse than jail food usually was, but ample. Apparently rationing hadn't yet started in Englor, in spite of the threat of war.

Most of what he could see around him matched what he would have seen in the average police station in London. The few differences were the more dramatic for that extra element of contrast.

The dress uniform (judging from the photographs on the walls) was white, with red stripes down the seams of the trousers. Along with WANTED notices on the bulletin board were a number of posters warning against loose talk, spreading rumors, and other wartime vices. Blade found particularly interesting one that positively screamed in foot-high letters "KEEP IT QUIET! THE ENEMY MAY BE LISTENING!"

The "listening" enemy was depicted as a barrel-chested, bearded blond peasant-type soldier, wearing a greatcoat and a conical fur cap with a leaping red flame emblem on the front. In his hands he carried an assault rifle with a large banana-shaped magazine, and half a dozen grenades hung from his belt.

Doubtless this was a caricature, no more accurate than wartime caricatures usually were. But Blade still found it intensely interesting, as an example of how the people of Englor saw the Red Flames of Russland, their enemies.

There was also something uncannily familiar about the poster. The rifle the Red Flame soldier was carrying seemed an exact duplicate of the AK-47, the standard assault rifle of the infantry formations of the Soviet Army! Another weird echo from Home Dimension.

On the wall directly behind the duty constable's desk hung a framed photograph, in the place where the portrait of the Queen hung in the police stations of Home Dimension. This photograph showed the head and shoulders of a man of about fifty, with dark hair going gray and a full beard. His face was square but fine-featured. He appeared to be wearing a military uniform tunic of some sort, dark blue gray with small shoulder straps and a high collar stiff with gold lace.

On the bottom of the frame was a small brass plate, and on it was engraved:

His Imperial Majesty Charles VI, Emperor and Supreme Protector of Englor

Blade's night in jail passed quietly, except for one noisy moment when a particularly quarrelsome drunk was brought in and deposited in the next cell. Morning came, a breakfast of coffee and sticky porridge came with it, and after breakfast two more police officers to escort Blade before the magistrate. He was given underwear, shoes, and a patched prison coverall. Then they hustled him into the same van that had brought him in last night and drove off.

Blade's was the first case on the morning's docket. Either the magistrate had a busy morning ahead or he didn't believe in wasting words. He was brisk, businesslike, thoroughly unsympathetic, and almost painfully precise in his speech and movements. Blade wondered if he starched his wig each night, to keep it so rigidly immobile above his long, thin face.

"Your offense is a serious one, sir. It shows a lack of any sense of decency or consideration for others. Such a lack is particularly reprehensible at the present time, when the Empire needs the most and the best that every man and woman can give."

The magistrate drew some papers toward him and cleared his throat. "Normally, I would impose the maximum sentence of ninety days without the option of a fine. However, you have not aggravated your offense by drunkenness, destruction of property, or resisting the arresting officers. You also appear to be an able-bodied and alert man.

"Therefore, I am going to offer you the option of enlistment in His Imperial Majesty's Armed Forces. If you volunteer, I will consider remitting half the sentence. If you are accepted for enlistment, the sentence will be entirely remitted. I shall also direct that your offense be stricken from the records, so that you may enter His Majesty's service without any stain upon your character."

The offer was an agreeable surprise to Blade, for several reasons. It gave him the chance to do something with his time in this Dimension, other than spending most of it doing whatever petty criminals did in Englor's jails. In fact, it gave him one of the best opportunities to study this Dimension that he could hope for, and above all to study its technology. With war hanging over the Empire, the armed forces would be getting the best its scientists and factories could produce, and as fast as possible.

There was a final reason why the offer was good news for Blade. It suggested that no one saw anything unusual or mysterious about his sudden appearance in the park, stark naked and in broad daylight. They might think he was not quite right in the head, but certainly no one seemed to be considering him a "man from nowhere," whose origins required a full-scale investigation. They seemed to be taking it for granted that he belonged here.

Enlistment in the armed forces wouldn't be all good news, of course. There would be all sorts of tests. There would also be an investigation into his background that might be sufficient to make someone suspicious.

Once he was in the army, there would be the usual boredom and idiocy of basic training. Even after that, he would not be as well off in Englor's army as he had been in a number of less civilized forces over the years. In civilized armies there was no chance to rise from private to general by catching the eye of the ruler or the ruler's wife. Without any education that he could prove, he would probably have trouble even getting a commission. He would very likely spend the war as a private or a corporal, and possibly without even a chance to distinguish himself in combat.

There was nothing he could do about any of this, however. He'd been given the best chance he was likely to get, and the only thing to do was take it.

The magistrate was staring hard at Blade, obviously waiting for an answer. Blade raised his eyes, met the magistrate's gaze, and said quietly, "My lord, I volunteer for His Imperial Majesty's Armed Forces."

Chapter 4

Blade passed all the physical and mental tests with flying colors. In fact he held himself back on all of them to avoid doing well enough to cause comment.

He was able to manage fairly well in presenting himself as a man without any past that needed to be checked out. He claimed to be a foundling with no known relatives, no friends, and no fixed place of residence for a good many years into the past. That still didn't account for a good many things, among them his excellent physical condition and the impressive array of scars on his body.

The induction officers and sergeants must have occasionally wondered about Blade, but they kept their wonderings to themselves. Blade thought he knew why. In the first place, any man so obviously fit and ready for service was a gift horse a wise man wouldn't look in the mouth. With war imminent, the officers and sergeants knew they'd be taking the lame and the feeble-witted before long. Richard Blade was one of the finest pieces of raw material anyone could hope for.

In the second place, the recent history of this Dimension offered a plausible explanation for Blade's skills, scars, and obscure past. Russland, the great enemy, had absorbed a number of small countries along its borders in the past two generations. In some of those countries, there had been little colonies of Imperial subjects. Many of them had been born in those countries and lived all their lives there.

When the Red Flames of Russland moved in, most of those from Englor died—killed in the fighting, executed, or starved and tortured to death in concentration camps. Those who survived lost homes and families and had to flee for their lives, suffering ordeals often too nightmarish to retell. A few of the bolder spirits remained behind and joined the guerrillas and underground movements in the various countries. Over the years, these became among the most formidable fighting men in the whole Dimension.

After a few days, Blade understood that he was generally assumed to be one of these ex-guerrillas. No one ever asked him directly, so he never had to give any specific information. He merely had to look reasonably wise when the history of those unhappy countries that were now Red Flame satellites was discussed.

Blade was tested and passed as fit for service at an induction center on the outskirts of London. Then he and thirty other recruits piled aboard a bus, under the eye of a large, beefy, but far from stupid sergeant. The bus took them to a railroad station, and the train they boarded there took them north to a training camp.

Blade did his basic training at a camp in the East Riding of Yorkshire—a name common to both England and Englor. They were not far from Whitby. In Home Dimension, Whitby was a fishing and coastal port and a resort town. In Englor it was the same, but it also supported a fair-sized base for the Imperial Navy and two airfields for the Imperial Air Force. Sailors, soldiers, and airmen on business or liberty packed the town's narrow streets, sometimes seeming to outnumber the local inhabitants. They gave the town a lively night life—sometimes a good deal livelier than the local inhabitants wanted.

At least this was what Blade heard from the soldiers at the camp who'd been there long enough to be entitled to passes. New recruits got none during the first six weeks of training. After that they got one evening pass into town every ten days. Blade never took his. He spent what free time he had devouring books and magazines in the camp library. When he absolutely couldn't stand the sight of tents and sandbags any longer, he would take a brisk, solitary walk along the nearest beach. This habit strengthened his image as a man alone, cut off from the rest of the world by a past he would not discuss.

The training was rigorous from the beginning, with the day starting at 5:00 A.M. and ending with "lights out" at 10:00 P.M. The hours between were filled with calisthenics, basic military courtesy, weapons training, testing for special skills, more calisthenics, more testing, and twice a week a twenty-mile route march with a fifty-pound pack.

The "square-bashing" or close-order drill that the British Army had always enjoyed so much was largely omitted from the training program. Blade mentally chalked up a large point in favor of whoever was in charge of the Imperial Army's training. They'd realized that there were only a certain number of hours in each day, and every hour devoted to close-order drill meant one less hour that could be spent teaching things more useful on a modern battlefield.

Not that the discipline was lenient. The drill sergeants and training officers came in all shapes and sizes, but they were all loud and demanding. Everything except eating, sleeping, and going to the bathroom was usually done "on the double."

Nor were living conditions particularly comfortable. The battledress was of such stiff fabric that it rasped the skin like sandpaper and was impregnated with something that smelled like an open sewer every time it got wet. All the clothing and footgear came in the two standard military sizes—Too Large and Too Small. Blade usually wound up with Too Large, something of a feat for the supply sergeants, considering that Blade stood six feet one and weighed over two hundred pounds.

The food was abundant, but the cooks seemed to believe there was something sinful or undisciplined about soldiers being able to enjoy their meals. So the meat was either burned black or half-raw, the cabbage stringy, the potatoes as hard as alloy-steel forgings, the tea indistinguishable from the water used to scrub the floors, and so on.

The barracks were new, which meant no vermin and only small pieces of plaster falling down on the recruits while they slept. On the other hand, the windows and the hot water hadn't been installed. Blade went to sleep every night with the breeze whistling past his ears, and woke up every morning to shave and shower in cold water.

After the first six weeks, the recruits went on from basic orientation on their rifles to marksmanship training. Blade made no effort to conceal his skill with firearms.

On the first firing for a rating, he shot 278 out of a possible 300. That was not only the highest rating in his recruit company, it was one of the three highest in the entire history of the camp. Blade found the rifle instructors looking at him with respect now, as well as curiosity.

Like any other modern force, the Imperial Army of Englor armed its men with a good many weapons besides their rifles. There were hand grenades. There were grenade launchers. There were the Uzis and two other kinds of submachine guns. There were launchers for firing half a dozen different kinds of small rockets, to demolish tanks, pillboxes, snipers, or low-flying enemy planes and helicopters. There were a dozen kinds of mines, demolition devices, and booby traps.

There was also map reading, camouflage, night movement and concealment, and all the other hundred and one skills that a modern army needed even in its private soldiers. Blade found it impossible to conceal all his great skill and comprehensive knowledge. This worried him at first, for it seemed likely to make him unpleasantly conspicuous. Then he realized that he would probably make himself more conspicuous and suspect by obviously holding himself back. So he stopped worrying and did his best.

His best was so impressively good that it was not long before even some of the sergeants could be heard admitting that Private Blade knew as much as they did and would know more before long. Blade knew it would not be much longer before he was tapped for an Officer Training Course. Hopefully the authorities would still consider him a gift horse, not to be looked at too closely. His status as someone who was probably an Englor refugee from the Red Flames would help. The authorities were usually more than happy to give such men the best possible chance to strike back at the Russlanders, whom they hated with a passion.

The weather grew slowly warmer. The recruits at the training camp began to join the regular units in the area for training exercises. Most of the exercises seemed designed to repel raids by Russland troops coming in from the air or the sea.

From all his reading and from listening to other men

talk, Blade now understood fairly clearly the military situation facing the Empire of Englor. It was not yet a crisis, but it could easily become one.

For all practical military purposes, Englor and Russland were the only two countries in this Dimension. Russland controlled the entire Eurasian land mass to about where the Rhine would have been. Englor ruled its home islands (including countries called Scotia and Airen) and a considerable overseas empire, including most of what passed for the Western Hemisphere and all of Africa.

There was nothing like North and South America across the "High Ocean," as the Atlantic was called here. There was one continent, about the size of Australia, and a great many islands of all shapes and sizes. Control of this overseas empire added a good deal to Englor's resources, but also even more to the territories it had to defend. Fortunately the Russland navy was substantially weaker than the Imperial fleet.

To the south and east of Englor's home islands lay something roughly equivalent to Western Europe. It was not quite the same shape as in Home Dimension, and it was a good deal farther away. The local "Channel of Englor" was over a hundred miles wide. The Nord Sea that lay between Englor and the precariously neutral Republic of Nordsbergen was more than five hundred miles wide.

If Englor was strong at sea and in the air, the Red Flames of Russland were immensely strong on land. Not surprisingly, the heart of Russland lay about where European Russia could be found in Home Dimension. But the Red Flames were a very different proposition from the Soviet Communists. They were an aristocratic and militaristic order, dedicated to war and conquest. They reminded Blade of the Teutonic Knights of medieval Germany. But the Teutonic Knights had collapsed in the early fifteenth century. In this Dimension the Red Flames had survived, prospered, expanded, come to rule all of Russland, and embarked on a course of expansion and conquest.

Over the last two hundred years they had expanded east, south, and finally west. During their expansion west they had absorbed nearly a dozen formerly independent countries and peoples. Their march of conquest had stopped for the moment at the borders of Gallia, but only because those borders were now defended by Imperial troops. Gallia's army was not large enough or well-equipped enough to meet the Russlanders in battle.

Now the march seemed to be underway again. The ultimatum over Nordsbergen was the signal. The mainland of Nordsbergen was about the size and shape of Norway and Sweden combined. On islands off its west coast, Englor had radar stations and air bases. The Nordsbergen people accepted those bases, knowing that their precarious "neutrality" depended entirely on them.

Now the Red Flames were demanding that Englor evacuate those bases. The next step after that would certainly be a Russland invasion of Nordsbergen. Then it would be the Russlanders who would have bases on the western islands, looking directly across the Nord Sea at the coast of Englor less than five hundred miles away.

A week after the field exercises began, the newspapers and radio announced that the Imperial government was accepting the Red Flame ultimatum and evacuating all facilities in Nordsbergen. There was a good deal of angry grumbling among the men in the camp when the news came out. There was also an increase in the training schedule, starting the very next day. After that no one had the energy to complain any more about the government's weakness.

Blade was quite certain that accepting the ultimatum had been no more than a move to buy time. Englor badly needed that time to mobilize and concentrate her army before war broke out. In the air and on the sea the Empire could match the Red Flames more than plane for plane and ship for ship, and with better planes and ships, too. On land, the Empire was outnumbered four or five to one. The Imperial troops were better trained and better armed, man for man, but there were not enough of them. The forces in the Home Islands and on the Gallic frontier would have to be reinforced by new recruits and men brought home from the garrisons abroad. Otherwise the Red Flames might very well overrun Gallia, destroying the Imperial forces there. Then Englor would stand alone, stripped of half her army and with her deadly enemies crouching on the coast of Gallia less than a hundred miles away.

Blade said nothing about his thoughts along these lines. He did not need any posters shouting LOOSE LIPS SINK SHIPS to be security-conscious. He'd learned his own security-consciousness in a school far harsher than the men around him had known, one they could not even imagine.

He was beginning to wonder if he'd ever have a chance in this Dimension to use everything else that he'd learned in that same harsh school.

Chapter 5

As the days passed, the training battalions at the camp went out more and more often on route marches and field exercises. Bit by bit they became familiar with the whole area between the camp and the Nord Sea coast, from Whitby well to the north.

It was a brisk, windy day, with scattered clouds scudding across a piercing blue sky. Blade's training battalion was marching along a narrow, winding road atop the sea cliffs about twenty miles north of Whitby. They'd been on the march since before dawn. Blade was beginning to look forward to the noon halt that was now only an hour and another three miles away.

Blade looked back along the double line of his platoon. He was now a Recruit Sergeant, and he stood a good chance of getting at least permanent corporal's stripes when he left the camp to join a unit. So far nobody had said anything to him about going to an Officer Training Course. Blade was half relieved at that, half disappointed.

His eyes wandered beyond his platoon, out over the sea. An army helicopter was skimming the waves, heading in toward the shore. A moment later Blade realized that it was heading directly toward the marching battalion. He followed it with his eyes as it whirred low overhead and landed near the head of the column.

A moment later the sergeant major gave the signal to halt. The battalion shuffled to a stop and waited, the men grateful for the unexpected break but also curious to see what it might mean. One of the NCOs at the head of the column ran across to the helicopter and climbed in. It rose into the air and swept back along the column, to land again a few feet from the cliffs, directly opposite Blade's platoon. The NCO jumped out, followed by two businesslike Military Policemen with ready Uzis. They strode briskly toward Blade's platoon, with an air of resolute purpose that Blade did not particularly like.

They strode directly up to Blade. He saluted. The NCO snapped, "Recruit Sergeant Blade!"

"Sir?"

"You are to accompany these sergeants. You are wanted for questioning."

"Sir!" Blade saluted again, suddenly alert and uneasy. Who or what had caught up with him, and how? What was the purpose of whisking him away from his unit like this, and in broad daylight, too? He could think of several possible reasons, none of them particularly pleasant.

"Very good, Blade," said the NCO.

Blade turned to the two sergeants, who had neither moved, spoken, nor relaxed their grip on their Uzis. "Am I under arrest?"

Neither of them spoke, but one of them blinked and the other shook his head fractionally. Blade realized that was all the answer he was likely to get out of them, at least here and now. In any case, there was no arguing with those Uzis. He shouldered his rifle and followed the two sergeants toward the helicopter.

They were airborne almost before Blade could strap himself into his seat. He leaned back against the vibrating wall of the cabin and tried to relax as much as possible. One thing somewhat eased his mind. They hadn't stripped him of his equipment or even of his rifle. Whatever they thought he was, it was apparently something not too dangerous.

Blade had no chance to ask any questions during the helicopter flight. The crew of the helicopter stayed in the cockpit, invisible from the cabin. The only people in the cabin besides Blade were the two MPs. He could hardly have talked with them even if they'd been willing to say anything, not in the cabin of a helicopter in flight.

Looking out the nearest window, Blade was able to roughly plot their course. For the first five minutes they flew due north along the coast, right above the beach. Then they climbed to about five hundred feet and swung inland. Blade saw the church towers of two small farming towns he recognized from exercises over the past weeks.

Then suddenly the helicopter was dropping like a stone, skimming low over the tops of a row of trees. The pilot cut the engine and they settled down to the ground. One of the MPs opened the cabin door and motioned to Blade to climb out. He picked up his rifle and obeyed.

Outside he found himself looking down the slope of a small hill to a grassy meadow beside a shallow stream. A twisting road, hardly more than an overgrown cowpath, ran across the meadow, passing over the stream on an ancient stone bridge. On the road just this side of the bridge was parked a gleaming black passenger sedan without any markings and an armored car with the markings of the Imperial Marines. The two MPs took position behind Blade and motioned him to descend the hill. He did so, aware every step of the way of the two gleaming Uzis pointed at his back.

At the bottom of the hill the MPs motioned him toward the sedan. Blade was conscious of a good many invisible eyes watching him as he walked across the meadow.

As he came up to the sedan, he saw that the door to the back seat was open, and someone was sitting in the seat. He took that as an invitation to climb in. He unslung his rifle, shifted it to his left hand, walked to the sedan, and started to climb in. Then he got a clear look at the man sitting on the far side of the rear seat, and froze in mid-movement. It took a very great effort of will to lock his suddenly numb fingers on the rifle so that it did not drop to the ground with a clatter.

Blade had expected to meet a long string of weird echoes of Home Dimension here in Englor. He had never expected to meet this one.

The man sitting in the back seat and now staring coolly at him had a black patch over his left eye. Otherwise, he was absolutely identical to J.

After a long pause, Blade completed the motions of sitting down on the back seat of the car, his rifle resting against the front seat. It was his body that completed the motions, without any help from his mind. His mind was racing off in other directions and into other places far from the sedan.

He'd more or less got over being surprised at finding in Englor duplicates of Home Dimension planes, buildings, cars, weapons, beers, and all the ordinary articles for living, working, and fighting wars. This was different. Somehow Englor had contrived at least a physical duplicate of a man who had been Blade's chief, mentor, and friend for many years. This was something so different that it was beyond Blade's power to avoid being shocked and stunned.

Slowly the shock faded, to be replaced by a quick series of ominous questions. Why had he been brought to this man? Was this twin of J also a spymaster, a power in Military Intelligence in Englor? If so, what could he want with Blade? Blade could not fight off an ugly suspicion that somebody had noticed something spectacularly mysterious about his origins and decided to take drastic action.

The man reached up to adjust the eyepatch. Blade noticed that there was a long whitish scar running up across the man's left cheek, disappearing under the patch. He also noticed that the man made the gesture in exactly the same way J would have done if *he* had been making it. The duplication of J seemed to go beyond mere physical appearances.

"Well, Mr. Blade. I rather imagine you're wondering why you've been brought here in this way?" The voice—and this was a relief—did not match J's. It was brisker, more clipped. Perhaps this man was younger than J, or perhaps he was simply less concerned about being a gentleman in all his relations with people, even those he might have to order shot in another five minutes.

"As a matter of fact, sir, I am."

"That's only to be expected. We sometimes have to use more—ah, dramatic—methods than we'd prefer. But we also sometimes have our orders, and not much more discretion in obeying them than a private in the ranks of His Majesty's Armed Forces. I can't blame you for being rather bewildered, but I hope you'll appreciate our situation."

The man's cryptic words explained practically nothing, including who were the "we" to which he referred so much. They did convey one very clear impression, however. This was the "soft" phase of whatever interrogation Blade was facing, with the interrogator pretending to be just another decent man who had to obey the orders of difficult superiors. Blade wondered when the "hard" phase—threats and abuse, or worse—would come. He was fairly sure that it would come sooner or later. Even the most civilized police and intelligence establishments used it, especially in wartime.

Blade decided to appear bewildered, but no more so than any reasonably intelligent man in his position would be. This man undoubtedly knew enough about him to know that he was not a fool. So it would be more dangerous than useful to attempt to play the fool. That would simply make the one-eyed man even more suspicious.

"As a matter of fact, sir, I don't—" he began. Then he noticed that the one-eyed man wasn't listening. After a moment Blade's own ears picked up what the other man was hearing—a peculiar deep-toned whistling roar that grew steadily louder. Then the other man was rolling down the window on his side and peering out. Blade did the same on his side.

An immense sharklike metal shape in Imperial Air Force markings and camouflage was drifting down out of the sky toward a landing spot in the meadow on the far side of the stream. For a moment Blade's mouth fell open in spite of himself, as the thought exploded into his mind that the scientists of Englor had discovered antigravity!

Then he realized that the approaching machine was simply a vertical takeoff and landing aircraft. He could make out the wings folded back against the fuselage, the bulges that held lift engines or swiveling nozzles for vertical thrust, the various complex devices for precise control in low-speed flight.

The VTOL transport was nothing new to Blade, but this particular one was something of a surprise. It was several times the size of any VTOL plane in Home Dimension. Its size and appearance implied technical breakthroughs well beyond anything in Home Dimension. Blade had access to even the most secret intelligence files on Russian and American developments in the VTOL field, and he knew. Nobody in Home Dimension could build a VTOL transport plane the size of a Boeing 747 and able to land as lightly as a June bug in an unprepared open field.

The huge plane settled gently, its belly opened to sprout an impressive array of landing gear, and it touched down. The howl and whistle of its engines faded away as they cut out one by one. A large nose hatch opened, dilating like the lens of a camera, and a jointed metal loading ramp unfolded itself to the ground.

Blue smoke puffed from the exhaust of the armored car. It began to move, rolling up across the humpbacked little bridge and across the meadow toward the plane. The one-eyed man reached forward and tapped the sedan's driver on the shoulder. The sedan's motor purred to life.

It was obvious that the armored car and the sedan were both going to be loaded aboard the transport and carried off somewhere. Blade didn't like the idea. It suggested that he was in the hands of people who could casually tap the latest and most advanced military resources of Englor for any job they wanted done. Ordinary intelligence establishments seldom had that power. Did the Empire have some all-powerful secret police organization lurking behind the scenes?

Blade felt rather than saw the movement behind him. He started to turn, but he could not turn fast enough. A long tweed-clad arm seemed to explode toward him from the other side of the car. In the large hand at the end of that arm was a gleaming cylinder—a hypodermic needle or spray, Blade knew. He also knew that he was going to be just a bit too slow to avoid it. He still tried to twist clear, one hand lunging for the door handle. But the one-eyed man had thrown the locks on all the doors. There was no way out.

Blade had just realized that when the hypodermic shot its load into the back of his neck, and all awareness drained out of him in a few seconds.

Chapter 6

Blade slowly became aware that he was in a bed, with sheets and blankets under and over him and pillows piled high under his head. A hospital bed? No, the usual combination of sterile, antiseptic hospital smells was missing. This room smelled of fresh air and flowers, like a guest room in a comfortable country inn.

He opened his eyes. What he saw confirmed the impression of the smells. The room was large and sunlit, with French windows on one end that gave a view of well-kept green lawns and flower beds, with trees and a lake in the distance. It was furnished with the bed, two large armchairs, a writing desk and chair, a small table, and a large antique wardrobe. There was restful green carpeting on the floor and wallpaper in a subdued floral pattern on the walls. The room was comfortable, without being luxurious.

Blade sat up in bed, threw off the blankets, and examined himself. He was wearing pajamas, blue silk ones that fitted as if they'd been custom-tailored. In its own way that was as impressive a demonstration of the resources of the people who held him prisoner as the big VTOL transport plane.

Blade had no doubt that he was a prisoner, although from the room around him he might have concluded that he was more of an honored guest. The French windows were undoubtedly wired with alarms and bolted inside and out, while concealed surveillance devices were just as undoubtedly monitoring his every movement, if not his every breath.

Blade climbed out of bed, took off the pajamas, and examined his body for signs of what might have happened to him since the one-eyed man knocked him out. He could find no cuts, bruises, burns, or even needle marks.

That didn't prove that nothing had happened to him, of course. Skilled interrogators could reduce a man to a whimpering wreck without leaving any traces on his body. By using spray injectors they could fill him full of a dozen different drugs without leaving a single needle puncture. He could have been broken thoroughly and pumped dry, then filled with amnesiac drugs so that he would not remember a second of the whole grim process. At least this could have happened if the people who held him were top-caliber professionals, and they probably were.

Examining himself again, he realized that he'd been shaved, bathed, manicured, and fed. So it would be nearly impossible to tell how long he'd been here from the growth of his beard or nails or how hungry he felt. He pushed the desk and one of the armchairs aside to clear a space in the center of the room. Then he went through a series of vigorous exercises to limber up and test for any loss of muscle tone.

He could detect none. Apparently he hadn't been a prisoner long enough to get out of shape. He continued with the exercises until he'd worked up a good sweat, then went into the bathroom. It was gleaming and modern, with a full set of towels, colognes, bath salts, and the rest. No razor or scissors, of course, but he'd hardly expected them. He stepped into the blue-tiled shower and turned on the water.

A hot shower left him feeling relaxed and ready for almost anything. He was toweling himself dry when the door clicked open and a woman walked in. Blade hastily wrapped the towel around himself and snatched a robe from the bathroom closet.

The woman paid no more attention to him than if he'd

been one of the pieces of furniture. She walked over to the bed and began making it with the brisk, practiced movements of the experienced housemaid. She wore a plain blue coverall, and from her face and graying hair Blade judged that she was about forty, neither seductive nor seducible. From the way she moved he suspected that she was both armed and combat trained.

Blade had no intention of trying to take the maid and use her as a hostage. At the same time he could never stop absorbing facts about his surroundings and drawing conclusions from them. He never knew when he might suddenly need something he'd learned that way. He did know that this habit had saved his life a number of times.

The maid went on making up the room, still paying no attention to Blade. When the last jar of bath salts was dusted off and placed back in the medicine cabinet, she finally turned to Blade. Her thin lips creased in an apparently sincere smile.

"Ah, Mr. Blade. You're awake."

Blade nodded. "I am," he said, matching her politeness with his own. It could do no harm.

"Very good, sir. I'll tell the Master. I'm quite sure he'll be happy to hear it." She turned and was gone before Blade could even begin to wonder, let alone ask, who or what "the Master" might be.

Less than five minutes later the door opened again and the one-eyed man entered. He walked with a brisk, military stride. It was a moment before Blade noticed that he also walked with a slight stiffness in the lower part of his right leg. Blade recognized that stiffness as the sign of an artificial limb. No doubt that was part of the reason for the revolver in the quick-draw holster under the man's left arm. He might be a bit slow on his feet, but there was nothing wrong with his hands or arms. Blade remembered the lightning stroke with the hypodermic and took care to keep his hands in clear sight as he sat down in one of the armchairs.

The one-eyed man drew up the other armchair and sat down facing Blade. Blade suspected that the distance between them was carefully calculated to be greater than he could cross before the one-eyed man could draw, fire, and hit him. The man looked like the type who would make that sort of calculation continuously and by instinct.

The man rested his left hand on the arm of his chair and looked at Blade. "Mr. Blade," he said, "my name, for the purposes of our conversation, is R. I am Director of the Special Operations Division of the Office of Military Intelligence of the Imperial Armed Forces. I am here to offer you a position with the Special Operations Division."

Blade kept his face carefully expressionless. "Perhaps you can tell me more?"

"Certainly. Regardless of the various unknowns in your background, you seem to have the skills and instincts to make you an exceptionally fine field operative for the Division. I need not tell you that we are entering a period of desperate crisis for Englor. I rather doubt I need to tell you that men highly gifted for field intelligence work are rare. In a crisis like this they are exceedingly valuable. I am offering you a position to which you seem well suited, where you can make an exceptionally valuable contribution to Englor's fight against the Red Flames."

Blade was astonished. About the last thing he'd expected was such a blunt offer of a position as a secret agent in the service of Englor, and from Englor's chief spymaster! What had they learned about him—or *not* learned about him—that made them willing to make this offer?

Blade leaned back in his chair and crossed one leg over the other. "I take it that you've—" He was about to use the phrase "interrogated me," but thought better of it. "—that you've examined my qualifications as thoroughly as you feel is necessary." A cumbersome phrase, but neutral.

"Yes," said R. There was a crisp finality in that single word that told Blade a great deal. It told him that he had indeed been interrogated, that they'd found out a great deal about him, and that he would never learn what they'd found out, no matter how many times he asked. In fact, asking would be not merely a waste of time, it would be dangerous.

Blade very badly wanted to know how much he'd said. Above all, he wanted to know if he'd revealed that he was from another Dimension. He might not have said so in plain words, but this was a scientifically advanced Dimension. Its interrogators could interpret his words and draw conclusions from them in ways that men from a world of swords and castles never could. Revealing his origins to these people would amount to revealing the Dimension X secret, and to people who might be able to make use of the knowledge. Blade did not know how advanced Englor's computer technology was. He suspected it was uncomfortably close to that of Home Dimension.

It was maddeningly frustrating. *How much did these people know?* Blade knew that he was a difficult subject for interrogation, but he also knew that any man can be broken, given enough time and the right techniques.

Well, if he wasn't going to find out, he wasn't going to find out. In any case, the odds were somewhat against their having dug out anything dangerous. That would have certainly required more than the few days at most that he could have been under interrogation. Also, there was R's offer of a position as a field operative. It seemed hard to believe that a "mystery man" or a traveler from another Dimension would be casually offered such a position—at least by an intelligence professional like R.

Blade set his mind more or less at rest and nodded. "Very well. It's certainly an appealing offer. May I ask—is there any penalty for refusing?"

R smiled and shook his head. "None whatever. Well, perhaps a slight one. It will cause less talk if you do not return to your training unit. So you'll be passed as fully trained and assigned with the rank of corporal to the Royal Yorkshire Light Infantry. Their field battalions are all with the Eighth Army in Gallia. No one in the Yorkshires will know there's anything unusual about you, and there will be a cover story for the men in the training battalion. We aren't interested in coercing you, Mr. Blade. We want you as a free agent, or not at all." A lift of the gray eyebrows told Blade that the pun was intentional.

"I see." It was not hard to decide what his answer should be. He was being offered a chance to spend his time in this Dimension doing exactly the same type of work he'd done in Home Dimension for years. He'd done it well then, he'd do it well now. It was also the best opportunity he could hope for to dig out whatever useful secrets this Dimension might hold. Finally, it would be interesting, and Blade was a natural adventurer who hated boredom almost more than he did armed enemies.

"Do you want an answer now?" he said.

R nodded. "If you feel yourself in a position to give one, yes."

"I accept."

R smiled, rose to his feet—slowly, but quite gracefully. He came over to Blade with his hand outstretched. Blade rose and they shook hands.

"You'll have to pass through our regular training course, naturally. I don't imagine that someone with the qualities you've shown will fail, however. So, Mr. Blade, I think I can say with some confidence—welcome to the Special Operations Division."

They shook hands again, and R opened the door. As he went out, the maid entered, pushing ahead of her a wheeled cart with an array of covered dishes, glasses, bottles, and pots.

Blade sniffed the various odors, and suddenly realized that he was a good deal hungrier than he'd thought.

Blade was again face to face with R only six weeks later. He spent the first three of those weeks in what was nominally the "training course." After the first few days it became obvious that he was not being taught the skills he would need as a Special Operations agent. He was being tested to see if he already had those skills.

That suggested they knew or suspected something unusual about his background. Refusing to worry about that, Blade concentrated with grim determination on passing every one of the tests as impressively as possible. There were tests in marksmanship and parachuting, weapons and vehicle maintenance, unarmed combat, swimming and scuba diving. There were tests of his reaction times, analytical abilities, stress tolerances, memory, and every other quality that it was possible to measure. There was testing ten and sometimes twelve hours a day. It was a grueling routine, but the beds were soft, the food was good, and Blade's iron constitution and machinelike endurance did the rest. No one, least of all Blade, was surprised when at the end of the three weeks he was declared to have passed all the tests by a wide margin. In some of them he'd made the highest scores ever recorded in the school.

He spent another three weeks learning things a little less basic, such as ship and aircraft recognition, Red Flame military customs, the use of Russland weapons, and the like. The Russland language was as nearly identical to Home Dimension Russian as the language of Englor was to Home Dimension English, and Blade spoke competent if not fluent Russian. The language instructors said he would have trouble passing as a native Russlander, but no trouble at all passing as a citizen of one of the conquered satellites.

While Blade was in training, the Red Flames were busily setting about adding Nordsbergen to their empire. Or at least they were arranging things so that they could move in any time they wanted to, in force, with no danger of facing effective resistance.

Their surface ships and submarines swept across the shallow Baltan Sea that lay between Russland and Nordsbergen, and out through the Straits of Gratz into the Nord Sea. They completely ruled the coastal waters of Nordsbergen. Landings were reported on a number of the islands along the coast. Fortunately, all the troops and equipment of Englor had already been evacuated.

In the air, Russland planes were over Nordsbergen twenty-four hours a day, flying low, flying high, buzzing cities and military installations, watching everything that went on, doing little damage but making a thorough nuisance of themselves. They were reported to be concentrating heavily over the high range of mountains in central Nordsbergen.

Here in the training school Blade didn't have to keep his mouth shut on matters of strategy, tactics, and politics. "There seem to be good sites for radar stations all along the range," he said. "With long-range sets up there, the Red Flames could extend their warning network halfway across the Nord Sea."

"That could very well be it," said one of the instructors. "We've had reports of Russ experiments with large prefabricated domes. They could be used for housing radar sets.

The Imperial Navy and Air Force made no effort to interfere with Russland operations over and around Nordsbergen. At the same time, they left nothing undone to keep a close watch on those operations. The Imperial Army was wasting no time either. Battalions and brigades arrived from overseas areas of the Empire almost every day. Other battalions and brigades crossed the Channel to join the Eighth Army facing the Red Flames on the eastern border of Gallia.

There was good reason for these troop movements. The Russlanders were steadily reinforcing their own armies in their satellite countries. In a single week eight new divisions were identified by Imperial Military Intelligence, three of them armored divisions. A mighty mass of men and tanks and guns was gathering opposite the Eighth Army, outnumbering it at least three to one. Against that kind of odds, even the better training and better weapons of the Imperial Army might not be enough. There was a race on between Englor and the Red Flames, a race to see who would be the first to be ready to strike. It was by no means certain that Englor was going to win that race.

At the end of the six weeks, the instructors at the school declared Blade fit and ready for a field assignment. He was ushered into a paneled office in the administration building of the training center, to find R facing him from across a vast polished desk. Spread out on the desk were a map of Nordsbergen and a number of files and photographs.

Blade scanned them briefly, then met R's eye. He could read nothing in that eye. That was familiar. J always held himself in, blank-faced and expressionless, when the time came to send a man out on a mission. R was the same.

"The instructors have been most impressed with your progress," said R. "They feel you're entirely ready for a field assignment. You've come along remarkably fast, all things considered."

Blade knew there would be no point in showing he

knew perfectly well he'd been tested, more than trained, these past weeks. R might not entirely appreciate knowing that Blade was that perceptive. Blade didn't want to risk even the slightest delay in leaving on his first mission for Englor. He felt trained and ready to the point of impatience.

"This is your first assignment," said R, making a sweeping gesture that took in all the material on the desk. He folded up the map and scooped everything into a leather case, then handed it to Blade. "Study all this thoroughly, memorize the map and the codes, and call me back within forty-eight hours."

They shook hands and Blade went out. As he passed down the corridor, he found that he had to force himself to remember this was not Home Dimension and the man he'd just left not J. He found his mind settling into the familiar patterns of preparing for a field mission, patterns well established in the years he'd worked for MI6.

Well, this was his original profession, the one where he'd shown his skills and made a name for himself. This was field intelligence work, with only the names changed from what he'd done for MI6.

In a sense, perhaps this *was* home—as much of a home as he could ever hope to have until he retired, if he lived that long.

Chapter 7

Blade's mission was to land on the mainland of Nordsbergen and pick up certain key files that had to go out by a covert route. He was not told exactly what the files were, but there were enough clues in the briefing material so he could make a good guess.

The files were probably a complete list of Nordsbergen citizens who would be willing to assist Imperial intelligence operations against the Red Flames, even after the country was occupied. That meant a complete list of the bravest and toughest people in Nordsbergen, and the most valuable to Englor. It was obvious why it had to go out by a covert route. There couldn't be even the slightest risk of its falling into Red Flame hands. That would sign the death warrant of everyone on the list, crippling Imperial intelligence operations in Nordsbergen for years. It would also destroy much of the confidence anyone in Nordsbergen might still have in the Empire's wisdom, judgment, and reliability.

Blade was not sure that committing such critical data to paper had been a wise move. He kept his opinions on that to himself. He also kept to himself his opinion that the Special Operations Division was mounting a fairly elaborate operation to take one man into hostile territory and take one file out. However, he knew all to well that even the most professional of intelligence chiefs occasionally overreacted, or had to obey superiors who did.

Once Blade was fully briefed, a helicopter flew him to Whitby. From there a fast motor launch took him and his gear ten miles out to sea, to a rendezvous with an Imperial atomic submarine.

The trip aboard the submarine across the five hundred miles of the Nord Sea took two days. That was probably a leisurely cruise for this submarine. It closely resembled Home Dimension nuclear submarines that could travel three times as fast without strain.

Blade studied the submarine as thoroughly as time and the need to avoid arousing suspicion permitted. She was small—two thousand tons or so, with no more than fifty officers and men in the crew. Blade saw nothing that it would have surprised him to find aboard a submarine of the Royal Navy in Home Dimension. If any technological breakthroughs had filtered down to the Imperial Navy of Englor, they were lurking in places where Blade could not see or recognize them.

Blade spent most of his time studying his maps, photographs, and equipment, or resting to keep up his strength. When he did go into action, he knew he would have to allow for at least forty-eight hours with no sleep and probably with little rest of any kind.

While Blade slept on the second night, the submarine rounded the southern end of Tagarsson Island and entered the channel that lay between the island and the mainland of Nordsbergen. Shortly before midnight her navigator's reckoning indicated they'd arrived at the correct position. The engines were cut back to dead slow, and the submarine settled quietly down on the bottom of the channel, so gently that Blade didn't even wake up. He slept until the petty officer in charge of his equipment shook him by the shoulder.

"Time, sir."

Blade sat up, bowing his head to keep from cracking it on the pipes above the bunk. He swung his legs out of the bunk and stood up, instantly awake. He could feel the familiar sensations of mind and body coming to full alertness for action. It felt as good as ever.

"Very good," said Blade. "What's the weather like up top?"

"Report is clear, ceiling and visibility unlimited, wind south-southwest at ten to twelve, light chop." The petty officer went out, closing the door behind him as Blade turned to the hanging locker on the bulkhead and began pulling out what he called his "working clothes."

Around Blade the blueness of the chill water was turning to green. He slowed his rise and exhaled more vigorously than before. Coming up from two hundred feet down had to be done slowly and carefully. Otherwise he'd reach the surface with his lungs ruptured, to bob away on the current as a slowly stiffening corpse.

He watched the luminous dial of his wristwatch until he saw that three minutes had elapsed. Then he began kicking slowly and steadily with his finned feet. The green around him grew lighter and still lighter. At last his head broke water.

He looked across the three miles of water toward the shore, getting his bearings. To his right rose Hugar Point, a headland rising sheer nearly two hundred feet from the sea. To his left a range of heavily wooded hills marched away into the blue distance, dark green against the sky. In the middle of the shadows they cast across the water,

Blade could make out a strip of whitish sand and the whiter curl of foam as little waves rolled up on it. That beach was his goal. Blade raised his other hand and took a precise bearing with the compass strapped to that wrist. He carefully looked over water, land, and sky with equal thoroughness, looking for any sign of human activity.

He didn't expect to find any. He was nearly twenty miles from the nearest Nordsbergen town, a fishing community of no more than a thousand people. There were a few farms and logging camps nestled among those hills, but none of their people would be paying much attention to the sea or what might rise out of it.

The Russlanders had no bases at all within a hundred miles. Even their nearest anchorage was forty miles away. Their air patrols passed over this area from time to time, but on a schedule that was predictable to within half an hour.

That was typical of the Russlanders. They were very thorough and conscientious in executing previously laid plans. They were also rather unimaginative in drawing up those plans, and slow to adapt to any situation not covered by the plans. This was a set of military vices very familiar to Richard Blade, and one he knew very well how to exploit.

Blade examined the little world that he could make out from mid-channel until he was quite sure no one was watching. Then he ducked down below the surface again.

The little electric torpedo was floating a few yards away, stabilized just below the surface by its buoyancy tanks. He gently pulled on the trailing line until he could reach out and grip the torpedo itself.

It was five feet long and eighteen inches in diameter, a fiberglass cylinder with controls forward and a rudder and propeller aft. It could carry Blade through the water at six knots for about ten hours. After that, if he needed to travel farther across the sea, he would have to inflate the life raft that was strapped to the torpedo.

Blade lay along the back of the torpedo, shoving his feet into the stirrups on either side of the rudder. One gloved hand moved to the controls. The propeller whispered into life and the torpedo began to glide forward through the green water.

Blade angled down until he was running thirty feet deep. He opened the throttle and felt the buffeting of the water increase against his arms and legs. He was aware of the chill of the water around him but not bothered by it. His dark green wet suit was as efficient an insulating garment as he'd ever worn, and his greased hands and feet felt no more than a faint nibbling from the cold.

He kept the torpedo on course at full speed for twenty minutes. The channel ran deep, with water a hundred feet deep only fifty yards from his beach. He hoped there would be a level place for him to park the torpedo that was also deep enough to make it invisible from the air.

When he'd counted off twenty-three minutes he slowed to half speed and began looking ahead and down, watching for the bottom to rise out of the dimness to meet him. At twenty-six minutes he saw it take shape, gray under the blue green around him. At twenty-eight minutes he cut the throttle completely. A moment later the torpedo settled onto firm sand forty feet down. Blade made sure that it was safely in place, then swam up to the surface.

To his relief he was no more than twenty yards from shore and a hundred yards south of the end of the beach that was his goal. He dove back down and started up the torpedo again. A few minutes at low power, and he set it down on the bottom again. This time he unhooked the anchor and dug it firmly into the sand. Then he unfastened the raft and the waterproof equipment pack from the torpedo and swam slowly toward the beach.

He swam until the water became too shallow. Then he began to walk, feeling out each step with his fins and meanwhile trying to look in all directions at once. For the twentieth time he told himself that the ideal soldier or secret agent would have eyes not only in the back of his head, but in the top and the sides as well!

Blade watched the trees on the shore with special care. For the moment he was virtually helpless in the face of an ambush, his torpedo out of reach, his raft uninflated, and no weapons ready for use except the sheath knife on his belt.

Nothing happened. He made it to the shelter of the trees and kept going for another fifty yards, until he was out of sight of the beach. Then he unslung his scuba gear and shoved his two packs out of sight under a bush. With his sheath knife he cut a branch from the bush, walked back to the beach, and with the branch brushed out his tracks. Now even a beach patrol would not easily realize that a man had come out of the sea and hidden in the forest. With that out of the way, he was finally able to strip off his wet suit and start unpacking his weapons.

He did not stop until they were all out and ready for use. A submachine gun, not an Uzi but another model with a folding stock and a barrel extension that could be screwed in place to give extra range and accuracy. Four fifty-round magazines of caseless 9-mm rounds. A flare pistol and six flares. Six hand grenades. Two knives, razor-sharp and balanced for throwing.

Blade checked all the working parts of the gun, then inserted a magazine and chambered a round. As it clicked into place he let out a sigh of relief. Now he was in shape to give anything short of a platoon of infantry a fight the survivors would remember all their lives. He hoped it wouldn't come to that. His mission depended on stealth and silence and speed, not on firepower and cutting down enemies in swaths. But it was never a good feeling to be nearly helpless, and it was always a happy moment when that helplessness came to an end.

Blade propped the gun ready to hand against a tree and stood up. Between the cool shade of the forest and sitting still in his damp underwear, he felt chillier now than he'd been in the water. He exercised for five minutes, made a quick tour of the area, then exercised for another ten. By the time he'd finished exercising, he was as limber as he needed to be and as warm as he could hope to be. He sat down again and started digging rations out of the pack.

He planned to keep most of the rations in reserve, in case he did have to spend a few days in the raft. But he needed some food now, to replenish the energy he'd used up making it to shore. He unwrapped chocolate and meat bars and began nibbling.

Over the next half-hour Blade slowly nibbled the ration bars down to crumbs. Then he carefully squeezed the foil wrappings into tiny balls, stowed them away in his pack, and relaxed. The courier with the files was not scheduled to make his appearance at the northern end of the beach until two hours after sunset. Sunset today was at 8:23. It was now just before eleven in the morning. Blade had nearly twelve hours of waiting in front of him.

Waiting, however, was another of the agent's skills that Blade had learned very thoroughly.

Chapter 8

Blade spent most of the day safely out of sight in the forest, sitting with his back to a tree and the submachine gun across his knees. Every hour he got up and made a quick patrol through the area around his hiding place. He didn't expect to find anything unusual or dangerous. He did want to make sure he knew the area better than anyone who might possibly sneak up on him.

Every two hours he slipped down to the beach and spent half an hour watching the channel and the sky above it. Once he saw three planes go over, three white vapor trails against the blue sky with a tiny metallic glint at the head of each trail. Both Imperial and Red Flame planes might have equally good reasons to fly high over this stretch of disputed land and water.

Another time he saw three fishing boats come down the channel, their engines puffing out blue smoke and their crews on deck laying out nets and buoys for the night's fishing. Blade scanned the boats from stem to stern with his binoculars, checking for signs that they might not be what they seemed. The Russlanders had taken over a good many Nordsbergen fishing boats and were using them to patrol the waters, which were rapidly becoming their private preserve.

Most of the confiscated boats were only lightly armed, so Blade doubted they could interfere directly with his mission. But they might put landing parties ashore, which would be a nuisance. They could also radio for help from the strong Russland naval and air forces only an hour or two away. That could be worse than a nuisance. Russland antisubmarine tactics were crude, but with overwhelming force against a submarine caught in shallow water they might be unpleasantly effective. Blade did not want to have to sail five hundred miles across the Nord Sea, bobbing along in his raft and living on ration bars and raw fish.

The men aboard these fishing boats looked like ordinary Nordsbergen fishermen who'd been sailing out after the herring and the cod for thirty years. Blade watched until they were out of sight, wishing he could do something to make it certain they could go on sailing out peacefully for *another* thirty years.

The late morning turned into early afternoon. The early afternoon turned into late afternoon, and the sun began to sink down toward the peaks of Tagarsson Island. The sunlight washing over the sea and the forest began to turn from yellow to orange and then from orange to red, slowly fading as it changed.

The light went swiftly after the sun sank behind the peaks of Tagarsson Island. A blue darkness settled down upon the sea and the forest, rapidly turning black. By nine it was nearly dark. Blade screwed the extension onto the barrel of the submachine gun. The extension tripled the gun's effective range. Now he could command the whole beach from end to end and a respectable stretch of sea as well.

He also pulled the infrared monocular viewer out of his pack and adjusted it. With the viewer to one eye he could scan his surroundings for infrared traces—including the signals from the IR lamp his courier would be carrying. Blade examined the whole beach with the viewer, noticing the wavering patterns that showed where the day's sun had heated the sand unevenly. He swung the viewer out to sea, examining the chill waters of the channel. Then he put the viewer away and again settled down to wait.

At a quarter to ten Blade pulled on his wet suit. Having it on might save him a valuable minute or two on his way back to the submarine. Then more waiting.

Ten o'clock came and went. Five minutes, ten, fifteen. So far, so good. Nothing seemed to have happened to hurry the courier on to the rendezvous. Blade picked up the IR viewer, scanned the beach once more, then looked out to sea.

Suddenly he stiffened. Out on the seaward horizon to the south was an unmistakable heat source, large, steady, and slowly but surely growing. Blade kept the viewer trained on the source until he could identify it as the hot gases streaming from the funnel of a ship. A good-sized one, too, and coming fast. Blade adjusted the range-finder element of the viewer and took a reading. Less than six miles off now, and coming on at twenty knots. It would be off the beach in less than twenty minutes and within striking range of the submarine in less than that. It was already within gun range.

A Russland destroyer. There couldn't be anything else that large and moving that fast in these waters now. Nordsbergen's coastal trade was suspended and its ships all tied up at their docks. Blade remembered what he'd read about the three most numerous classes of Russland destroyers. All of them packed speed, firepower, and detection equipment enough to make them formidable opponents even for the most advanced Imperial submarine under the right conditions—such as shallow water.

If Blade tried to escape now with the torpedo or the raft, the destroyer could pick him up on its sonar or radar and probably eliminate him as easily as a lizard picking flies off a rock with its tongue. If he stayed on shore, the destroyer could send a landing party large enough to comb the forest for him. They might not catch him, but they could certainly drive him far inland, away from the sea that was his road home.

Perhaps the destroyer's arrival was a coincidence? Blade doubted it. The Russland hadn't been running any regular surface patrols through the Tagarsson Channel.

Yet suddenly here was a destroyer coming straight at him. No, it was here for a purpose, because somebody among the Russlanders had heard or suspected something.

What had they heard and how had they heard it? Blade knew that it would be enormously valuable to find out. He also knew that there were a good many other things he would have to do first, including getting out of here alive!

He pulled on his combat webbing and slung the raft and survival pack on his back. He might not have to move far, but he would almost certainly have to move fast and be ready to shoot at any moment.

His gear rode comfortably, and seventy-odd pounds plus the submachine gun was an easy load for him. He looked at the beach again, paying particular attention to the forest at the far end. That was where the courier was scheduled to appear and give the coded recognition signals with his own IR lamp.

Then Blade was off, moving inland until he was sure he was invisible from the sea. After that he swung north, moving parellel to the beach and covering ground as fast as the forest would let him. Every few yards he went to cover and listened silently for any signs of human movement in the darkness around him.

He wanted to be at the north end of the beach when the courier arrived, so the man wouldn't have to signal. There would certainly be infrared scanners about the destroyer, and an IR signal from the courier would reach more people than Blade. It would be a loud cry of "Here I am!" to the lookouts aboard the ship.

The courier might also have some Russlanders on his trail. That could mean a nasty shoot-out, and in that case the more cover the better. The destroyer would be less able to tell one side from another and join in at long range. No doubt the captain would eventually make up his mind to send a landing party, but Blade and the courier might have plenty of time to get clear before then. Blade was determined to get the courier out as well as the file, if at all possible. The man might be able to give useful information about affairs in Nordsbergen, perhaps including how the Russlanders had got wind of the rendezvous and pickup operation. It would aslo eliminate any chance of his being captured and questioned before he could commit suicide.

No sounds came from the forest around Blade, no light or movement. Once he swung back toward the beach to take a bearing on the approaching ship. It was now close enough to make out with the naked eye. A low-lying dark silhouette, with squarish turrets forward and aft, two squat funnels, a tall tripod mast—unmistakably one of the Russlanders' fleet destroyers. Still coming fast, too, judging from the growing curl of white at her bow. Blade ducked back into the forest and moved on, faster than before.

At last he reached the north end of the beach and dropped down behind a fallen tree. The tree covered and concealed him from the rear, from the destroyer. The other three directions he wanted to cover himself, watching for the courier, the enemy, or both.

Minutes passed, each one seeming like half an hour even to Blade's disciplined mind and alert senses. His eyes were moving continuously over beach and forest and sea, and his hands held the submachine gun ready.

In those same minutes the destroyer out on the dark sea grew still larger, until she seemed as large and menacing as a battleship. Then the curl of white at the bow began to fade away as she slowed down. Now she was moving past the beach, about two miles off shore and barely maintaining steerageway. She would be practically on top of the submarine lying on the bottom.

That in itself was no real danger. The bottom of the channel was rugged, and more than one sunken ship lay down there in the cold dark water. It would take better sonarmen than the Russlanders usually had to tell one odd-shaped lump on the bottom from another, or one motionless metal hull from another. The submarine was safe, as long as she didn't move.

Unfortunately, it was equally true that as long as the submarine didn't move, she could do nothing against the destroyer or for Blade. Launching an attack from where she lay now would be a gamble, too likely to end in mutual destruction for both ships. That would leave Richard

Blade with a long, cold sea road home, if he got home at all.

A minute or two later, a faint sound drew Blade's attention from the destroyer to the forest toward the north. He raised the gun, flicked off the safety, and listened. The sound came again, a second time, a third. It was coming irregularly, confused and broken by the trees and the wind blowing through them, but it was hard to mistake. It was the sound of a man running fast.

If that man was the courier, it was not good that he was running. That could mean an enemy hard on his heels. Blade considered moving farther into the forest, to be ready to ambush anybody pursuing the courier, but decided against it. He already had the best cover and the best field of fire he was likely to find.

The sound of running feet grew louder. Blade listened to them, and also for any sound of pursuit. Except for the wind and the single set of racing feet, the forest remained silent. Either there were no pursuers close behind or they were moving so quietly Blade couldn't hear them.

Suddenly a man dashed out between two trees, into Blade's view. Blade snapped the submachine gun into position to fire one-handed from the hip. He raised his free left hand and made the six quick movements of the hand recognition signal. The man caught the movement, froze almost in mid-stride, and went flat on the ground. Blade could see that he had a blond beard and wore a field jacket and dark trousers. He had a light pack on his back and a holstered pistol at his waist.

Blade aimed the submachine gun directly at the man, waited a moment, then repeated the recognition signal. His finger was tightening on the trigger when the man slowly raised one hand and gave the proper countersignal. Blade saw that the hand was dark with dried blood. It was also shaking so badly that Blade could barely recognize the signal.

"Come on over," said Blade in English. The man started nervously, looked all around him, then quickly scrambled over to Blade on his hands and knees. He winced each time his bloody hand touched the ground. As he scrambled into cover, Blade could hear him gasping for breath. His eyes were wide and his face bleached to an unnatural white. It was a minute or two before he could even try to speak.

When he finally got the words out, they came in a rush. "They are right behind me, the Russlanders. Somebody gave them the rendezvous and the route. They ambushed us, hit me and Maria. I came away. They are coming only ten minutes behind, maybe." He shrugged off his jacket, wincing at the pain the movements seemed to awake in his arm, then reached inside the jacket with his good hand and tore at the lining. It gave, and a bulging plastic-wrapped envelope fell onto the dead needles. The man picked it up and handed it to Blade.

"Here. It is waterproofed. You must go now, before they come. If you give me that—" he pointed at the submachine gun "—I stay here, put some of them down while you get away. I take a few of them, for Maria."

"Who's Maria?" Blade asked. His briefing hadn't mentioned any such person.

"My wife," said the man briefly. "She come with me, because I need a second gun after the Russlanders started landing on our shore. I had to leave her behind after the ambush." What was in his eyes as he said this was far worse than any simple pain from a wound.

Blade hated the thought, but there was another question he had to ask.

"Was she alive?"

It was brutal, but Blade had to know if there was any chance the woman would be captured alive and made to talk. The man shook his head.

"No. Three bullets in her stomach and another in her head. She will not talk. Now you know everything. Go, please, now! It will all be wasted, otherwise." He reached for the submachine gun.

Blade kept a firm grip on it and shook his head. He hated even more telling the man that his troubles weren't over. Again there was no choice.

"I can't leave. There's a Russland destroyer out in the channel, just a couple of miles away. We can't move until something's done about it."

The man turned even whiter and his face crumpled up

as though someone had stepped on it. Then he put his face down on his arms and began to weep, silently but desperately.

Blade thought of breaking out thc first-aid kit and giving the man a sedative. But he didn't want to have to cope with an unconscious body along with everything else. As for slapping or punching the man to bring him around, Blade found he could not force himself to do that. The courier had obviously been through a nightmarish ordeal these past few days, and seeing his wife shot down before his eyes was only part of it.

In another ten minutes Blade at last heard the Russlanders approaching. It was hard to tell how many there were, but easy to tell that they had no fear of any opposition. They were tramping briskly along with a great thudding of feet and cracking of branches, shouting back and forth loudly in Russ. From time to time Blade heard the metallic clink and clatter of their weapons.

He picked up the file and checked to make sure the incendiary strip was in place. If he couldn't get clear, he could jerk the tab on one end of the strip and reduce the whole file to a charred and illegible mess in seconds. Then all he would have to worry about was not being captured alive himself, and he knew any number of ways to ensure that.

The approaching Russlanders seemed to have either stopped or quieted down. Now Blade could hear only an occasional footstep, and only once a human voice. He studied the woods. No sign of any worthwhile target yet. He wanted to wait until he could be reasonably sure of cutting down half a dozen with his first burst. That would—

In the distance, Blade heard the unmistakable cracking roar of heavy guns firing. A whistle sounded high in the air, rising to a scream. Blade turned in time to see a pillar of sand, gravel, and smashed trees rise from the far end of the beach. He ducked as bits of steel and wood kicked up sand all along the water's edge.

The courier jerked all over, buried his face deeper in his hands, and gave a faint whimper. Blade suspected he knew well enough what was happening, so that there was no need to tell him. The destroyer was going to bombard the beach and forest. The two of them might be blown to bits. Certainly they would be pinned down until their pursuers could launch an attack.

More shells, landing inland. Still more, on the beach but closer to where Blade crouched and watched. In the gun flashes the destroyer was clearly visible, almost dead in the water. Bow and stern turrets were firing alternately, hurling a salvo toward the land about every thirty seconds.

Two shells landed well short of the beach, throwing up tremendous pillars of silvery water. Then four shells burst almost together, raising a sheet of yellow orange flame and sending a wall of sand and smoke sweeping toward Blade. He closed his eyes and ducked down again, protecting the raft with his body. The last thing he could afford now was a puncture in it.

More shells, closer still, tossing a full-sized tree end over end into the air. It splashed down into the water as another salvo came in. The ground seemed to heave under him, the fallen tree jumped several feet into the air and fell back again, and shell fragments sailed past in a weird chorus of pipings and whistlings.

Before the chorus died away, Blade's mind leaped ahead, to realize where the next shells would land—if the destroyer's gunners kept to their pattern. Being Russlanders, it was better than even odds they would. The price of guessing wrong would be death for Blade and the courier, but at least it would be a quick death.

Blade tossed the raft over the tree and grabbed the courier by the collar. Half heaving, half pushing, he pulled the man to his feet and sent him sailing over the tree, to land on top of the raft. The whistle of incoming shells sounded in Blade's ears as he made his own leap. Their explosion caught him in midair. Somehow he managed to hit the ground in the shelter of the tree before the air was filled with enough flying steel to have torn him to shreds. Somehow he also managed to land holding the muzzle of the submachine gun up out of the sand. Beside him the courier lay full-length, as silent and nearly as stiff as a corpse. Blade kept his head down, too dizzy from the concussion to be able to rejoice that he'd guessed right.

There was silence for a moment, then more shells whistled in. Explosions crashed again, and Blade had to roll clear as the tree bounced several feet toward him. If he hadn't moved, it would have landed across his legs. He lay there, his hearing slowly returning, aware that blood was running from his nose, aware also that he was waiting for a particular sound. He knew it almost had to come.

It came. From the forest where trees now lay tossed and tumbled in mad heaps came a thin chorus of screams. The Russland gunners had carried their pattern too far, landing a full salvo squarely on top of their own infantry patrol. Blade looked over the tree, which was now well chewed on both sides by shell fragments. He could see a number of khaki-clad figures sitting or sprawling among the fallen trees. Someone staggered to his feet, raised a submachine gun, and let off a stream of tracer into the sky. He wasn't shooting anywhere near Blade. Apparently he was trying to signal the destroyer. Blade raised his own weapon and squeezed off a five-round burst. The Russlander fell back out of sight, his gun falling with him. It went on spraying tracer until the magazine ran empty, then fell silent. Once again the only sound Blade could hear was the moaning of the maimed and dying.

Beside Blade, the courier staggered to his feet. The sight of the smashed forest and the dying Russlanders seemed to restore both his wits and his courage. He turned to Blade and grinned savagely. "Nice shooting, for us, yes?"

Blade nodded, sprang over the log, and motioned the other man to follow him. They had to close in now and finish off any surviving Russlanders. Then they would have to get inland, away from the destroyer's guns and from the landing party that would almost certainly come ashore the moment the captain realized what had happened.

The courier was just sliding down to squat beside Blade when a machine gun went *tak-tak-tak* off to the right and bullets went *wheeeet* past Blade's ear. He dove for the ground, the courier only seconds behind him. Blade saw the courier spin around, drop to his knees, then collapse, blood flowing from chest, shoulder, and right arm.

Without raising his head, Blade pulled out his first-aid kit, then crawled over to the courier. The man had half a dozen bullets in him, and he was going to die without much better care than he could get aboard the submarine. That was obvious at a glance. Blade still worked furiously, disinfecting and injecting and bandaging. If the man would just live long enough to tell how he had been betrayed to the Russlanders—

The machine gun fired again. Apparently the gunners could no longer see the two men lying on the ground and were firing at random to pin them down. Then the destroyer could range in on them, and this time there would be no mistakes with the target. Blade soberly wondered if either he or the courier had much chance of living more than another ten minutes.

Again a burst from the machine gun. This one went on so long that Blade guessed they would now have to change belts. He risked raising his head enough to look out to sea. Then he stared in surprise and mounting delight.

The destroyer had come about and was heading away to the south, down the channel. White water at bow and stern showed that she was already doing twenty knots and working rapidly toward full speed. A big searchlight forward was sweeping the sea in a great arc. Something sudden and compelling was drawing the destroyer away from the victims waiting for her on land. Blade didn't know what this could be, but he didn't have to. What he did know was that for the moment all he faced were the machine gun, its crew, and perhaps a handful of other Russlanders in shape to fight. Dispose of them—and quickly, because the destroyer's captain might turn back or a helicopter arrive with reinforcements. Then inflate the raft, get the courier into it, paddle out into the channel, signal to the—

A sheet of yellow flame tore upward from the destroyer's stern. On top of the flame rode a crown of flying pieces of the ship—depth charges, steel plates, boats, men, the whole after turret with its jutting guns and radar gear. At the base of the flame the sea rose in a dark wall topped and laced with foam. Then the thunder of the explosion came rolling across the water. Blade thought he'd become used to explosions by now, but this one swelled and swelled, until he had to open his mouth and clap his hands over his ears. The ground under him vibrated, and several weakened trees cracked and toppled over.

As the flying pieces started splashing back into the sea, Blade saw the machine gun clearly. The two gunners had both risen to their feet and were staring open-mouthed out to sea, blind to everything except the dying ship. They paid no attention to Blade as he pulled a grenade from his belt, jerked the pin, and threw it. The men still had their mouths open when the grenade landed between them, so they died that way.

Two more Russlanders sprang up from cover as the blast of the grenade died away, but Blade was ready for them, his finger on the trigger. A quick burst and the two men went down. Blade waited another minute, looking for anyone still able and willing to make a move against him. At last he was satisfied there was no one left.

As he turned back toward the sea the wave from the explosion struck the shore, a six-foot wall of green water and foam. It rolled up the beach, scouring away the craters from the shells, reaching high enough to catch several fallen trees and pull them out to sea as it drew back.

Blade looked down at the courier. The man was still breathing, but deeply unconscious. Probably just as well, considering his wounds. Blade picked up the raft and survival pack and carried them down to the water's edge. Returning, he picked the courier up in his arms and carried him down to the shore. The man weighed over a hundred and sixty pounds, but to Blade's muscles and adrenalin-charged system he seemed light.

Blade unpacked the raft and jerked the inflation tab. The CO_2 cartridge went off with a *wssssh* and the five-foot doughnut of dark rubber rapidly filled and firmed out. Blade laid the courier in it, making him as comfortable as possible. Then he pushed the raft through the shallows until it was well afloat, sprang in, and unfolded the paddles.

The raft moved slowly and sluggishly with the extra weight aboard, and it had only a few inches of freeboard. But it showed no sign of being unstable, and that was enough for Blade. The raft didn't have to take him and the courier back to Englor. It just had to keep them afloat long enough to be picked up by the submarine.

Five hundred yards offshore Blade looked toward where the destroyer had been. At first glance she seemed to have vanished completely. Then Blade saw a long, low, rounded shape in the water, moving gently to the swell. The light from a patch of burning oil a few hundred yards away showed red paint on it, and a few tiny dots perched along it. The destroyer's stern was gone, blown to bits. The bow was still floating, capsized, and with a few of the crew clinging to it.

A thousand yards farther out, Blade shipped the paddles and began laying out three hand grenades. Three grenades exploding at one-minute intervals was the agreed-upon signal for the submarine to surface and make pickup.

Blade had the first grenade in his hand, ready to pull the pin, when a long, thin metal tube slowly crept out of the sea two hundred yards away. A faint wake trailed away behind it. Then the wake died, the tube rose higher out of the sea, and the rest of the submarine followed the periscope. Foam swirled away from the stern as the officers on the bridge maneuvered their ship toward Blade.

A line darted across the water from the three sailors standing on the deck. Blade caught it and pulled the raft in hard against the gleaming black steel of the submarine's hull. The sailors moved cautiously down the hull toward the water until they were practically hanging on their safety lines. Blade sprang up lightly from the raft onto the hull, and all four men joined together in heaving up the raft.

Blade let his breath out with a long sigh of relief, saw that the three sailors were gently lifting the courier, and headed for the bridge ladder. There was one more thing to be done before he would be satisfied with the night's work. As he scrambled up onto the bridge, he saw the submarine's captain leaning against the railing, binoculars around his neck.

"Welcome back, Mr. Blade," said the captain.

"Thank you, sir," said Blade. "Now, if you can manage it, I think we'd do well to pick up a prisoner or two from that destroyer."

The captain shook his head. "I'm sorry, Mr. Blade. It might be useful, but it would also be dangerous. We can't afford to stay around here much longer, and certainly not on the surface."

"But—"

"No, I'm sorry. We were able to get rid of that destroyer only by using—by using something we didn't expect to have succeed so well. I'm not going to risk my ship any further, now that we've got you aboard." He smiled politely but turned away with a finality that suggested he would not be polite if Blade pushed the matter any further.

Blade shrugged. Both he and the captain were right, in different ways. The captain was right in not wanting to endanger his ship any further. On the other hand, a prisoner or two from the destroyer might tell Englor much, possibly even something about their ship's mission.

But aboard his own ship there was no arguing with the captain. There was nothing to do but accept his decision and hope the courier lived to talk.

The diving alarm hooted. Blade stepped aside to let the lookouts and the officer of the watch plunge down the hatch, then followed them.

Chapter 9

The captain might have been reluctant to risk his ship to pick up prisoners, but nothing else seemed to bother him. He took the submarine north and snaked her through a narrow and little-used channel just north of Tagarsson

Island. Clear of coastal waters and Russland patrols, he ordered flank speed, and the submarine raced out across the Nord Sea. The turbines whined, the decks vibrated, and things not fastened down crept across tables and decks.

The mad rush took them across the Nord Sea in fourteen hours, but that wasn't fast enough for the courier. He regained consciousness once, long enough to know where he was and to hear Blade tell him of the destroyer's sinking. That made him smile in deep satisfaction—three hundred or more Russland sailors gone in return for his wife. It wasn't enough to save him. An hour later he lapsed into unconsciousness again.

The submarine pushed on, eventually surfacing five miles off Whitby. Then a helicopter was called, and the courier and Blade were loaded aboard it and flown to a hospital.

The courier was dead when they took him from the helicopter.

R wasted no time. He arrived to debrief Blade only three hours after the courier's death. Blade found himself whisked off to a "secure" room and kept there for the next twelve hours. Blade kept going—he was determined not to let a man so much older than he was outlast him. Besides, he was used to such exhausting debriefings. J's fondness for Blade had never let him be easy on the younger man in professional matters. R was a man cast in the same mold.

After Blade had finished telling every detail of his mission at least five times, R called an end to the debriefing and ordered in a meal. Blade went through the steak-and-kidney pie, grilled mutton chop, Brussels sprouts, and gooseberry tart with cream as if he were eating his last meal. Then he poured himself a cup of coffee and leaned back in his chair, full, content, relaxed, and quite ready for anything else that R might throw at him.

R pulled out cigars, offered Blade one, then lit one for himself. After a few puffs he fixed Blade appraisingly with his one eye.

"I was under the impression we'd handed you a fairly

straightforward mission, Mr. Blade." He seemed to be expecting a reply.

Blade nodded. "I was under that impression too." He matched R stare for stare. "I don't think I can be held responsible for the complications, though." His omitting "Sir" was deliberate. It was high time to learn a few things from R. Not what Special Operations already knew about Richard Blade—that would always be out of reach. But he might learn something about what they were planning on doing with Richard Blade in the future.

"Not for the complications that actually took place, perhaps," said R. "But what about your bringing out the courier? What about your request that the submarine try to pick up survivors from the destroyer?"

They'd been over these points before. Blade knew that, and he also knew that R knew it. Presumably R had some particular purpose in pushing the matter. That didn't make it any less annoying, and Blade didn't see any reason to go on concealing his annoyance. He didn't have to give the impression that he would tolerate being treated like a child. So when he spoke, his voice was clipped and as chilly as liquid oxygen.

"We've been over that several times, sir. I doubt if there's any profit or purpose in doing it again. The courier stated in plain English that the network in Nordsbergen had been blown. It seemed likely that he might be able to give useful information on how this had happened."

"Why not interrogate him yourself?"

Blade realized that R was asking the question in perfect seriousness. "As it happened, it was impossible. We had too many—ah, unexpected visitors, of one sort or another." The phrase drew a thin smile from R. "Even if we hadn't been busy fighting, I would have preferred to bring him out. It would have been better to have him interrogated by someone who knew more than I did about the background of Imperial intelligence operations in Nordsbergen."

"Such as myself?" said R.

Blade nodded. "In any case, the courier was hit. I could have tried to take a prisoner from among the Russland wounded, but I don't think any of them were in much better shape than the courier. That would have also meant leaving the courier behind. I wouldn't do that."

"And the destroyer's survivors?"

"The average deckhand probably wouldn't know why his ship was where it was. But an officer who knew something more might have survived. It seemed worth investigating."

"Not to the submarine captain, though."

"No, not to him. I'm not sure either of us was really in the right *or* in the wrong. We had different missions, and so we thought along different lines."

"You think the submarine had something to do other than deliver you and pick you up?"

There was nothing in R's voice to give a clue to anyone less perceptive than Richard Blade. To Blade, R's polite question blazed like a signal flare, lighting up things that had been in the dark until now.

No, not quite in the dark. For at least six hours out of the past twelve, Blade's intuition had been raising a pointed question. Had his mission been a real one, or—something else? Blade decided that it was time to trust his intuition and put that question to R.

"Yes. I think the submarine's mission was the real one, and I was being sent ashore as part of a diversionary operation. I rather imagine that what the courier died bringing out was a fake, while the real material came out by some other route." Blade kept his voice neutral. He was too experienced an intelligence professional to get indignant over this sort of deception, although he'd never liked it and never would.

"What was the submarine's mission, in that case?"

"I imagine it had something to do with the device they tested successfully against the destroyer. From what I saw, I suppose it was a high-speed decoy that would match the acoustic and sonar profile of the submarine. They launched it, waited until the destroyer dashed off after it, then fired a high-speed acoustic torpedo straight up its—stern."

There was a long silence in the room while R stubbed out his cigar and lit another one. Then he smiled. "The

Imperial Navy wouldn't be at all happy to learn how easily you guessed what they were doing."

"And you?"

"I'm entirely happy with practically everything you've donc or said. You acquitted yourself extremely well. Agents with ten years' experience have done much less well in the face of considerably weaker odds. You've obviously got a great natural aptitude for this sort of work."

"Thank you, sir."

"Don't thank me for my good opinion of you until you've seen what it will lead to. You'll be assigned as an Independent Operations Specialist. That means one lonely assignment after another, usually deep in enemy territory. You'll go out on those assignments, one after another, until you start losing your edge or the Red Flames kill you. You won't be finding much pleasure in life."

"I didn't expect that I was being invited to a year-long party," said Blade with an edge in his voice. "I expected a great deal of dangerous work, and perhaps a short life. I also expected that it would be of some service to the Empire."

"My apologies," said R, and he seemed to be speaking sincerely. He reached into another drawer of his desk and pulled out a decanter of whiskey, a soda-water syphon, and two glasses. "I've said it before, Captain Blade, but I think I can properly say it again. Welcome to Special Operations."

"Thank you, sir," said Blade. "Captain?"

"You need military rank, otherwise you'll be neither fish nor flesh nor fowl to the more orthodox military types. Captain isn't really high enough, but it's as high as I can get approved for somebody of your rather modest seniority.

"You won't be a captain very long, however. There will be quite a few vacancies at higher levels as soon as we know which of the present Independent people will have to be transferred out of fieldwork. Some of them haven't made the necessary adjustments from peace to war."

Blade nodded. That was inevitable, in any intelligence network. Even some people who had already been living and working under near wartime conditions couldn't go on when the world marched off to war all around them.

They sipped at their whiskey, and R went on. "As far as our operations in Nordsbergen being penetrated, we've suspected that was the case for several weeks. So we set up a number of diversions at the ends of all the routes we suspected might be compromised. Each of these diversions was also covered by another operation. Meanwhile, we set up a completely new route to extract all the key material and personnel. It worked quite successfully."

"What about the diversions?"

"We sent in six of our people. You are the only one who's still alive."

Blade could not come up with a quick or easy answer. R saved him the trouble.

"We also suspected this would happen when we heard that General Golovin was in Nordsbergen."

The name rang a faint bell in Blade's mind. "Their security chief?"

"Yes. The Chairman of the Counterintelligence Office of the Red Flames' Administration of State Security. He's a professional soldier, but he's made a specialty of intelligence work for thirty years. He personally directed Red Flame operations against Imperial citizens in three of the conquered countries over the last fifteen years."

"He must have come up fast. Is he that good?"

"He is. He's also a thoroughly unpleasant type, personally. A sadistic streak a mile wide. He also has one other weakness. He's too fond of being as far up front as he can manage when there's a big operation on. Since he's six feet eight, he's rather hard to conceal. So when he's spotted, it's usually a reliable indication that the Red Flames have a high-priority operation underway. We can react accordingly."

"I see." R's being able to react on cue had been no help to five of the six agents who'd been part of the reaction. But that was too often the way intelligence operations worked out. Knowing who your enemy was and where he was didn't necessarily mean safety. It could mean that he knew the same things about you.

"Do we have anything on *how* the Nordsbergen operations were blown?"

"Nothing reliable. We're doing a good deal to remedy that situation, of course, including checking for leaks in our own staff. That will be one of your jobs for about the next six weeks."

"Sir?"

"You'll have about six weeks of light duty before you start the briefing for another field assignment. During that time you'll be assigned to Division Headquarters. You'll be one of the first new people there since the crisis with the Red Flames developed. That means you've a good chance of being one of the people any Red Flame agent will test out, to see if you can be used. I trust you have no objections to keeping a watchful eye on your colleagues and associates?"

Blade slowly shook his head, and gave the answer he'd worked out for himself over the years. "No, sir, I can't say that I do. In the long run it's self-defense. If they're working for the opposition, they can kill me just as thoroughly as a Russlander with an assault rifle."

R nodded, smiling, and poured out some more whiskey.

Chapter 10

For three days Blade was assigned a private room in one wing of Special Operations headquarters. Except for the view and the different color scheme, the room was identical to the one in which he'd awakened on his first day in the service of the Division. During those three days it was made clear that he not only didn't have to do anything but shouldn't even try.

The medical officer was blunt. "It's a pattern we're trying to break. Tough young man does four field jobs in rapid succession without resting up between them. Thinks he's indestructible. Sneers at doctors' orders to rest. Goes out on fifth mission and stress load catches up with him. End of tough young man." He glowered at Blade through thick-lensed glasses. "With a war on we can't afford this, even if you think you can."

So Blade spent three days catching up on lost sleep, missed meals and intelligence reports that had come in while he was out in the field. He didn't mind three days of it, but he was glad it ended before boredom set in.

He spent a number of hours during those three days studying the files on the huge VTOL transport planes. Officially they were Avro Model 167 Assault Transports. Unofficially they were "the Elephants." Blade's status as an Independent Operations man gave him an acceptable "Need to know" for information about them, and about a good many more of the latest Imperial weapons and devices.

As Blade told the chief clerk, "I may be traveling in one of the Elephants before too long."

The clerk looked dubious. "Maybe, captain, and maybe not. They're lovely great machines, no doubt of it. But they've got a ways to go before anybody except the test pilots will be riding in them anywhere." Blade nodded politely, dropped the files into the attaché case chained to his wrist, and returned to his room.

The clerk had probably been giving him a cover story. The existence of the transports could not be kept a secret, so somebody must have decided to do the next best thing—give out a story that they were still full of bugs. Blade was quite certain that the assault transports were much closer than that to being ready for combat.

After reading the files, he was even more certain that the Empire had to be saving the Elephants as a nasty surprise for the Red Flames. It certainly would be a nasty surprise when it came. The big planes could carry fifty tons of cargo or two hundred fully equipped soldiers two thousand miles, land vertically, unload, take off vertically, and return to base. They could exceed the speed of sound at low altitude and move even faster higher up. The variable-sweep wing helped give them an incredible combination of speed, range, and maneuverability.

As Blade expected, these qualities required a number

of technological breakthroughs. At least three new alloys were involved in the construction of the assault transports, all superior in strength-to-weight ratios and heat resistence to anything else in existence. So was a new chemical fuel, five times as powerful as the best of conventional jet fuels.

There was no hard data in the files on either the alloys or the fuel. Blade didn't expect to find any. The fuel and the alloys were undoubtedly classified several degrees beyond MOST SECRET. It would be a long time before he would be able to prove any "Need to Know" for them.

It took time, though, to build the factories and refineries to produce the new alloys and the new fuel. Until these were ready, the assault transports would have to remain experimental and secret. After that, they could be turned out fifty or a hundred each month, instead of two or three. Then the Empire of Englor would be able to fly whole divisions thousands of miles and land them in the Red Flames' vital areas. Then the Red Flames would have to worry about every square mile of their immense territories. Englor might never land a single soldier inside Russland. But the fear that they might do so could keep hundreds of enemy leaders awake at night and hundreds of thousands of enemy soldiers tied up on local-defense duties. The whole balance of the war might shift in Englor's favor.

After the three days of rest and reading, Blade was assigned to his light duty. This meant more reading of more files, four to six hours a day. It also meant occasional administrative decisions. Some were routine, some not. There was one occasion when he was asked for a decision on whether a certain pro-independence politician in one of Englor's African colonies should be assassinated. Blade advised against it.

"There is no compelling reason for doing so at the moment," his memorandum read. "The loyalty of the African units has not been seriously impaired. We are more likely to impair that loyalty by making Case 28 a martyr than by leaving him alone."

Blade hoped that recommendation would do some

good. He wondered, though. The fact that he was allowed to handle files and make recommendations might mean that no one in Special Operations suspected a thing about his origins. But he had no way of knowing how many levels there were between him and the real decision makers. He didn't know if he was actually functioning in isolation, continuously watched for some revealing slip. He didn't know a great many things, and while he was resigned to this situation, he still didn't like it.

One thing he knew was that the more background he got, the less likely he was to make slips. So he read files the six hours a day his duties required, and another six or eight hours each day on his own. He could only hope this would look like conscientiousness, rather than a desperate effort to learn things he should have known as well as he knew his own name.

One evening he was sitting in the Senior Lounge, a glass of beer on the floor beside his armchair and a file on Russland electronic countermeasures spread out on his lap. He became aware of someone passing in front of him and looked up in time to see a young woman sit down in the armchair on the opposite side of the little alcove. For a moment Blade pretended to be looking at the painting hanging on the wall over the woman's chair—what looked like a vintage 1900 battleship at sea, pouring out great clouds of smoke and firing her guns furiously in all directions. Then he saw that the woman was looking directly at him, stopped pretending to ignore her, and returned her gaze.

He recognized the woman as someone from the Headquarters staff, but this was his first good look at her. Short, but carrying herself so well that she looked a good deal taller. Excellent figure, shown off to advantage in a gray tweed skirt and a maroon blouse, and very good legs. Hair cut in a neat pageboy bob, so blonde that it seemed to shimmer against the dreary wallpaper and even drearier upholstery of her chair. Large, intensely blue eyes, and a wide mouth that began to curve upward into a gentle smile as Blade watched.

"Good evening," she said. "I've seen you around here a

few times, but we've never really been introduced. My name's Elva Thompson."

Blade smiled, acknowledging her polite frankness. "I could say very much the same thing."

Her smile extended itself to her eyes. "Does that mean that your name is Elva Thompson, too?"

Blade laughed. "No. It means that I've seen you here several times too, but— Anyway, my name is Richard Blade."

"Oh yes, you're the newest of the Independents, aren't you?"

Blade spent a moment considering how she might have discovered that fact. He did this more by reflex than because of any real suspicion. Here in the headquarters, where practically everyone had a Grade One or Two security classification, there were few secrets about who was doing what. When, where, and how were another matter.

"Yes," said Blade. "You're on the staff here, somewhere."

She nodded. "I'm Assignment Coordinator for Staff Personnel."

Blade was impressed. Elva couldn't have been more than thirty, but her position was the second most important one for the day-to-day running of the headquarters. It was her job to keep track of staff assignments and shift people from one to another as circumstances demanded. That meant a Grade One classification, since she had to know a good deal about at least the planning end of every major Special Operations job.

Elva's eyes fell on the files spread out across Blade's lap and on the rug beside his chair. "Am I interrupting something important?"

"Not really," said Blade. "I was beginning to think of tidying this up and tidying myself off to bed." He looked at his watch. "It's getting toward eleven, and I'm doing refresher jump training tomorrow. The alarm will be going off about five."

"You're going to jump in on your next mission?"

Blade shook his head. That might be a perfectly normal and innocent question. He was still glad that he could give a perfectly polite answer that revealed very little.

"Not necessarily. You know the way we Independents get pushed around. Forty-eight hours' notice, all of it spent getting briefed. Then off we go, to some place whose name we may not even know until we get there. That means we've got to keep up every skill that we might possibly need."

"I see." She seemed to be hesitating, even a little nervous for a moment. Then she continued. "Do you suppose you could get me on one of the jump-training flights?"

"To jump?"

"Yes. I've got my own gear."

"Are you planning to apply for a place among the Independents?" said Blade.

Elva laughed. "Oh no. I know my limits. I'm competent enough, but not that athletic. I'm also too sociable to spend my working hours perched on top of some frozen mountain in Russland, with nothing more intelligent than a sheep for fifty miles. It's just that skydiving used to be a hobby of mine. Now the fuel allocation for civilian flying has been cut down so far that it's hard to get someone to take me up."

Blade knew what Elva meant. Bit by bit, the Imperial government was forcing the people of Englor to tighten their belts. Food, fuel, all sorts of consumer goods were slowly being restricted. Full-scale rationing was at most a few months away.

"I don't think I can do anything for you this week," said Blade. "There's too heavy a training schedule. Next week, on the other hand—well, I'll see what I can do."

"I can't ask for more than that," said Elva, with a smile that seemed to light up the alcove. "Except perhaps if you would care to buy me a drink?"

Blade looked at his watch. It was now past eleven, and he'd been awake and on the go since well before six. On the other hand, he no longer felt tired or sleepy. Perhaps it was the effects of Elva's company? In any case, a drink with her suddenly seemed like a very good idea.

"I'd be delighted," said Blade, and rose from his chair to take Elva's arm.

Chapter 11

They had to wait a week, but then there was no problem about slipping Elva onto the flight schedule for three jumps. Blade said only that Elva was "considering" applying for field training. "Considering" was a noncommittal word—she could always say afterward that she'd changed her mind, if any bureaucrat seemed likely to make a fuss. Probably none would. Special Operations was run with a refreshing lack of red tape. R knew perfectly well that the kind of people the Division needed for its work couldn't be treated like infantry recruits.

So Blade and Elva spent an entire day of the next week on the jump range. The weather was gray and drizzly in the morning, but in the afternoon the sun came out and made the last two jumps of the day pure pleasure. Blade loved skydiving and warmed to anyone like Elva, who so obviously loved it also.

She not only loved it, she was really good at it. She was in excellent condition, skilled and even graceful in all the movements of leaving the jump plane, guiding herself down through five thousand feet of empty air, and landing safely on the green grass of the drop field. She not only landed safely, she landed as accurately as Blade.

As they were repacking their parachutes after the last jump, a thought struck Blade.

"Why don't we requisition a car and go into town for dinner? I don't know about you, but I haven't been outside the Security Area since I joined Special Operations."

"Except for that mission to Nordsbergen," she said quietly.

Blade nodded. "True. But that hardly counts as relaxation. The food was poor, the entertainment worse, and I couldn't say much for the company either."

Elva laughed. "I'll try to be better company than the Russlanders."

"I don't imagine you'll have to try very hard," he said. "Meet me at the garage at six?"

"Fine."

For the Military Reservation that held Special Operations headquarters, the "town" was York. The old city was much the same mixture of the familiar and the strange that no longer unsettled or confused Blade. He was still alert for any differences that might mean useful knowledge to take back to Home Dimension, or danger for him here in Englor.

Elva had been on duty at the headquarters for nearly three years, so Blade let her act as guide to the restaurants and night life of York. She did as well as she could, considering that there were only half a dozen good restaurants in the city. Fortunately it was a week night, so none of them were packed wall to wall with servicemen on pass.

They settled for a place called the Duke's Head. Blade wondered which duke in particular the name meant, but didn't ask. He didn't want to even hint at any strange ignorance of Englor's history, not to Elva. She'd been asking a good many questions about him and his work—too many for Blade's complete peace of mind. He wasn't suspicious of her—not yet—but he had well-developed instincts against telling anyone more about himself than was absolutely necessary. Those instincts were now fully alert where Elva Thompson was concerned.

They had one of the dining rooms at the Duke's Head to themselves and ate surrounded by dark oak, smoke-tinged red brick, and gleaming copper. The service was good and the food superb. Cheese soufflé, country ham with roast potatoes and young peas, fresh strawberries with thick clotted cream, a fine Gallic red wine, and an even finer brandy afterward—it was one of the most agreeable meals Blade could recall eating in any Dimension. He could not help feeling that it was rather a pity he had to be on the alert for whatever games Elva might possibly be playing. A pity or not, it had to be done.

Closing time was approaching. Elva looked into the bottom of her glass, where a few drops of golden brandy still caught the firelight. She seemed to be hesitating over something she badly wanted to say.

"Richard."

He reached for the brandy bottle. "More?"

She shook her head. "I don't think so." More silence. "Richard. Have you thought about our possibly spending the night here in town?"

"Tonight?"

"Is there a better night?"

"I can't say. Probably not, if—if this is what you want." Blade's own hesitation was only partly an act. Elva's question had reminded him of how long he'd been grimly set on doing his job and of how glad he would be of a chance to put it aside for one night.

"Why do you say that?"

"You know what my job is like, Elva. You know how many of the Independents have already bought it and how many more are going to. I think I'm about the last man around Special Operations you ought to let yourself care for."

Elva seemed to be touched by his concern, but also slightly amused. "Perhaps. But the risk is mine to run, if I want to run it. I won't tell you how to blow up missile bases if you won't tell me how to run my life. Fair enough?"

Blade knew when he'd met a woman who had made up her mind. He lifted his glass and emptied it. "Fair enough. Let's stop and pick up a couple of toothbrushes, then find a hotel."

The hotel lay with oak trees and gardens all around it, and night birds were singing when Blade and Elva drove up to the front door. Their room was on the second floor, with a window that looked out through the oaks and down the hill, across the countryside to the north. It was dark now, and there was nothing to see beyond the narrow fringe of light around the hotel itself. Blade and Elva would not have been paying much attention to the scenery in any case. They had a time and a place for themselves,

of the beautiful woman who stood before him, ready and waiting. He could only sense a breathtaking beauty and did not care about precisely what made it breathtaking.

Blade stood up and somehow managed to finish stripping himself without fumbling or delay. Somehow he reached Elva and lifted her in his arms. Somehow he carried her to the bed and placed her on it. The room was so warm that they did not need to crawl under even the top blanket. Probably neither of them would have done so even if the room had been as chilly as the night outside. It would have held them apart for a few more seconds, and that would have been too much time for either of them.

Elva lay down on top of the blanket, and Blade lay down on top of her. It was as simple as that. Blade moved deep inside Elva, and Elva twined herself around Blade and matched his movements with her own. At first they moved to separate rhythms, then the rhythms matched. They soared steadily toward the same goal, and they reached it in so nearly the same moment that neither could ever tell afterward who was first. Both could tell that the climax seemed to whirl them along with the terrible and beautiful force of an autumn wind whirling leaves through the air. Neither of them could tell anything for quite a long time after that.

Eventually they both realized that the room seemed cooler, even cold. It chilled the sweat that ran down Blade's neck and trickled down between Elva's breasts, and sent new and unpleasant shivers up and down both their spines. They crept under the blankets, and the warmth they felt then slowly built until another kind of warmth was once again flowing through them. When that warmth was at last exhausted, they slept.

Blade and Elva began their relationship with an intensity that could not have lasted even if they'd both had unlimited free time. Since both had jobs to do, there was only so much time they could spare for each other. Still, they made love again in the morning before returning to headquarters in time for a late breakfast. They were also able to snatch a night in town every ten days or so.

There turned out to be more time for them than Blade

had expected. Summer was passing and autumn not far off before he was called in for the first full briefing on his next assignment.

"Your mission will involve assisting an extremely valuable defector to get out of one of the satellites. You will have the assistance of as much of the underground in the area as may still be functioning at the time."

"General Golovin's been at work again?"

R grimaced, as if the cigar in his mouth tasted sour. "General Golovin, and also some of his handpicked younger colleagues. He's a good picker, so they're not to be despised any more than he is."

R gave up on the cigar and threw it angrily into the wastebasket without bothering to stub it out. Fortunately the wastebasket was nearly empty. One piece of paper flared up in a puff of blue smoke, then died out. "We also have a Probability Two estimate that there's a major leak within the Special Operations Division itself."

The Probability Scale ran from One, a nearly mathematical certainty, to Seven, almost impossible. A Probability Two for a major internal security leak was bad news. Blade mentally braced himself. He knew what the next question would be, and it also would be bad news.

"What is your best personal estimate of Elva Thompson?"

Blade let his breath out in a long hiss, while his mind swiftly assembled the most accurate words it could find. "I would say Probability Three that she is unreliable. I can't honestly give a Probability Estimate on whether she is unreliable for personal reasons or—political ones."

"After six weeks of your relationship with her?" R showed no signs of being concerned about the relationship itself, only about what Blade might have learned in it.

"Yes." Blade matched R's cool stare with one of his own. "I don't think this is the first time it's been hard to tell the difference between a gossip and a subversive."

R laughed shortly. "Well put, and quite right. However, I think you would agree that gossip can reach subversive ears much too easily. So I don't think we can take any more chances with Elva Thompson or several other people who are also under suspicion."

Blade would have been uneasy by now, except that R's voice held no hint that he was planning to haul Elva or anyone else before a firing squad. Apparently he had something less drastic in mind.

"Fortunately, we can kill a whole flock of suspect birds with one stone," R continued. "We are setting up a shadow Special Operations HQ in Norfolk next month. The dozen or so key posts will be duplicated, so that the new facility can take over part of the administrative and planning load—even all of it, in an emergency. We'll assign all of our suspect people to the shadow HQ. They won't be getting any plans or operations material for several months, so they can't do a damned thing, regardless of their motives."

"Meanwhile, a real shadow headquarters will be set up in still a third place?" put in Blade.

"Yes. Probably somewhere in Scotland. Norfolk's a little too close to the Nord Sea coast for comfort."

Blade nodded. R was handling the situation by one of the classic methods. The best way of handling a suspected enemy spy was not to simply eliminate him on the spot. That gave the enemy useful information about your security measures. Instead, you created a sort of administrative isolation booth for the suspect, keeping him there and seeing that he got nothing but false information. That not only told the enemy nothing, it could also deceive and confuse him.

"In due course, we will be able to tell whether any of the set of suspects we've reassigned were involved in the leak. Then we can tell whether we need to shoot them for treason or merely dismiss them for talking out of turn." R smiled at the last phrase, but it was an extremely thin and entirely mirthless smile. "Do you have any suggestions, Captain Blade?"

Blade shook his head. Regardless of what R had proposed, he wouldn't have said anything that might be interpreted as a plea to deal lightly with Elva Thompson. R's actual proposal threatened Elva with nothing worse than boredom, at least for the time being.

"Now," said R briskly. "Back to the matter of your forthcoming assignment." He raised into view a bound stack of envelopes as thick as the manuscript of a long novel. "This is the basic data. You have a full week to assimilate it, and I suspect you will be needing every bit of the time. Oh, one more point. I'm trying to put through your promotion to major. We have a few vacancies now."

Blade didn't ask how those vacancies had come about. He didn't need to know, and in fact he didn't altogether *want* to know. One thing he did want to know, however—

"Could you tell me what kind of defector I'm going to be dealing with?" That could make a good deal of difference in a tight spot. If the defector was a deadly marksman with the physique of a champion soccer player, he could be an asset. If he was seventy years old, half blind and totally deaf, he would be a very different proposition.

"It's a woman named Rilla Haran. She's the most brilliant of Russland's younger geneticists, responsible for some fundamental breakthroughs in genetic manipulation and large-scale cloning. Apparently she felt that she could no longer lend herself to the use of her discoveries for military purposes, so she— Captain Blade, are you listening to me?"

"Yes, sir." That was not quite correct. Blade was listening to R. He was also listening to an echo in his own mind—the echo of J's words as they walked along the corridor below the Tower of London.

"In genetics, we've had reports that the Russians are on the pointing of cracking the codes for direct genetic manipulation."

So now he was about to go off in search of a young lady from Russland who'd been doing exactly the same kind of work, and who carried in her mind—what?

No one in Englor knew at the moment. But he, Richard Blade, would be among the first to learn.

Chapter 12

Blade parachuted in on his mission to help Rilla Haran defect. His rendezvous with the geneticist lay in the satellite country of Rodzmania, on the shore of an inland lake three hundred miles from the nearest coast.

So Blade crossed into enemy territory at twice the speed of sound, fifty thousand feet up, aboard a strategic reconnaissance plane of the Imperial Air Force. He sat on a folding seat in the electronic warfare officer's compartment, watching the enemy coast scribble itself in glowing white across the dark radar screen, then slowly drift away behind them.

Twenty miles inland alarms *bleeeeped* fiercely, warning of enemy missiles on the way up. With the unpretentious coolness of an old hand at this sort of game, the pilot waited calmly as the six missiles closed at nearly three times the speed of sound. Then he launched the Number One decoy. The decoy was a miniature jet plane, as fast as the bomber for short distances and equipped to give off the same radar signal. The decoy raced off toward the missiles. Blade watched it go on the screen.

It met the missiles. Six proximity fuses activated six warheads. Decoy and missiles vanished together as explosions laced the frozen stratosphere with flame and flying metal.

The shock wave threw Blade from his seat to the floor. Before he could recover, the pilot was twisting the controls, sending the big plane plunging down through ten miles of sky to level off just above the treetops. Through the windows, Blade had a good look at the forests of Rodzmania hurtling toward him at six hundred miles an hour.

The pilot grinned. "We started down right after the explosion and went down fast until we went off their long-range radars. They probably think they got us. Even if they're wondering, it'll take them half an hour to organize a low-level search of the area. By that time we'll have dropped you and be on the way out. They don't have a really good radar network for tracking low-altitude intruders, so we shouldn't have too much trouble."

"Good luck," said Blade, with feeling. "I'm glad I don't have to do this for a living."

The pilot's eyebrows rose in wry amusement. "You could say that, I suppose. But then we could say exactly the same thing about your job."

"I suppose you could," said Blade, and left it at that. He did not look down on those men of war who fought their battles as part of complex teams of men and highly sophisticated machines. He respected their courage and their skills. But he'd long since recognized that he had very little in common with them. He was a man who fought best alone.

Blade looked at his watch. They would be coming up to the drop point in another ten minutes. He raised one hand in a final salute to the bomber crew, while with the other he opened the door leading aft to the bomb bay. It closed behind him, and he was alone with darkness and the distant thunder of the engines all around him.

Fifty feet aft was the bomb bay. Half of it was taken up by the massive cameras and sensors of the plane's reconnaissance equipment. Most of the rest was filled with racks of parachute flares, boxes of aluminum-foil strips for confusing enemy radar, and less-recognizable devices. At one end of the bay was a small folding seat, and above it hung Blade's gear.

He pulled it on, item by item—main and emergency parachutes, helmet, radio, survival pack, knife. He was jumping only with what he needed to take him to the rendezvous with the Rodzmanian underground. Even so, he was carrying an eighty-pound load by the time everything was in place.

The moment after he stood up, he felt the floor tilting under him as the plane banked to the left. They would be turning now, to make their approach to the valley where Blade would land. Then he felt the plane beginning to climb. The plan called for a jump from three thousand feet. The hills on either side of the valley rose five to seven thousand, so they would effectively shield the plane from enemy radar.

A sharp whistled sounded, and a light just above the seat flashed red. Blade climbed up on the seat, gripping handrails on either side. Light suddenly filled the bay as the doors swung open, and the roar of air passing at hundreds of miles an hour followed the light. Blade pulled his goggles down over his eyes and stared down at the panorama of pine forests and rock-strewn meadows passing below.

Suddenly his mark was there, the twin-peaked hill with the little lake nestling between the two peaks and the stream flowing silver out of the lake. Blade watched it sweep past and out of sight, counted to five, then let go of the handrails and plunged forward into space.

The air thundered deafeningly around him and the roar of the jets joined in. Then he was clear of the plane, falling free toward the ground below. He spread arms and legs to guide himself, watching the trees crawl past below without seeming to come any closer. For a long moment he was in the timeless, noiseless, weightless world of the skyjumper.

Then he passed two thousand feet, and the ground seemed to leap up at him. It seemed that he dropped a thousand feet between one breath and the next. He looked down again, saw that he was on target, jerked the rip cord on his main chute, and felt the reassuring, bone-wrenching jerk as it opened. He felt himself lose speed as the canopy filled, and then he was drifting down slowly, safely part of the world again.

He looked up. There was no dome of white or camouflaged fabric drawn taut above him. The parachute was made of an experimental material, almost completely transparent. Only the faint blurring of a circle of blue sky told Blade that he was not held up by magic. From a distance there would be nothing at all to see, either now or after he landed.

Far away to the north, he could see the fast-diminishing dot that was the reconnaissance plane. Even as he watched, it vanished completely. He knew that in about another ten minutes the plane would break out of the shelter of the hills on either side of the valley. Then it would register on enemy radar, and so would the decoys that it would be dropping.

Man-sized, man-shaped, dropping at the same speed as men, the decoys would leave any radar operator or ground observer firmly convinced that he was seeing a landing of spies or saboteurs. There would be an alert. There would be helicopters, armored cars, and infantry patrols rushing about, using up fuel, wearing out machinery, losing sleep. There would be a tremendous flurry of activity, none of it closer than a hundred miles to Blade's landing point, none of it anywhere near any of the underground's bases or any part of its network. There was nothing in the area where the decoys would be landing except mountains and forests and the mountain herdsmen and lumberjacks who lived in them.

Blade looked down again, saw that he was approaching a clearing, saw also that he was likely to drift right over it into the trees beyond. He pulled the shrouds on one side to spill some air from the canopy, and felt his descent quicken for a moment. That was enough. He came down two-thirds of the way across the clearing, landing so gently that he felt as if he were doing everything in slow motion. His parachute brushed against the branches of a pine tree and whispered down to the ground behind him. Then everything was still. Only the clouds crept across the sky above him, and only a faint breeze made small sighs in the treetops.

Quickly Blade gathered up the main chute and took off the emergency one. He carried both into the forest until he came to a small gulley drifted full of pine needles. He buried both chutes in the needles and brushed the surface over them as level as possible.

Then Blade walked back out into the clearing, took one bearing from the sun and another from the compass in his pack, turned his face toward the southeast, and started walking.

Blade was on the move for thirty-six hours out of the next forty-eight. He had sixty-three miles to cover, over terrain that held him to an average of less than two miles an hour. It was a matter of simple arithmetic to conclude that he had to keep going.

Blade moved steadily across the hills, with the agility of a mountain goat and with even more care for staying under cover. There wasn't much in these high, bare hills, but he used every bit he could find. There were not only the Russlanders to fear, there were the people of these hills, the herders and hermits who treated every stranger as an enemy. On the morning of the third day he walked down the last hill and five more miles through the forest, to his rendezvous with the Rodzmanian underground.

Blade's contact was a man named Piedar Goron, a logging engineer by profession. He could build or repair almost any building or machine that a logging camp might need—barracks, generators, spillways, even the great trucks that took the logs to the sawmills. A man that skilled had a good deal of freedom to come and go when and where he pleased, even under the rule of the Red Flames. Piedar Goron took full advantage of all that freedom, and a little bit more besides.

There were close to three hundred men in the underground network in this part of Rodzmania. Piedar Goron knew very few of them, and even fewer knew him. But he could give an order and know that it would reach all of them and be obeyed by all of them.

"The Red Flames may someday be able to figure out a way of dispensing with people like me," said Goron. "But first they will have to find people who are both loyal to them and who are good engineers. Either that, or they will have to shut down most of the industry of Rodzmania. Neither will happen before all of us are many years older."

Blade did not feel like replying. Whatever the Red Flames could or could not do in the end would make no difference to Piedar Goron. A man who put his life in danger as often as Goron did could not expect that life to be very long. Five years? Perhaps, with luck. Two years seemed more likely. If Goron had any children, they might live to see Rodzmania liberated from the Red Flames. He himself never would.

Goron handed Blade a mug of beer and drew one for himself. There was silence in the hut until both mugs were empty. Then Blade put his down and said, "Very well, I'm here. What do *you* say is next?"

Blade's briefing had covered a dozen different plans. He also knew that the choice among them could safely be made only with the help of the man on the spot.

Goron leaned back against the wall of the hut and lit his pipe. He made such a prolonged business of it that Blade began to suspect bad news. Goron only spoke after he'd taken several long draws on the pipe.

"There is no way any more to take you and Rilla out along Route Green. Two days ago the Russlanders sent a battalion of security troops into Dungorad and arrested nearly four hundred people."

"How many of our—your people were among the four hundred?"

Goron shrugged. "The network in that area was so thoroughly disrupted that we do not even know that. I suspect we lost enough so that those who were not taken are lying very quiet for the time being. There might still be enough to support Route Green. But if the people are too frightened to even send reports, they will certainly be too frightened to help bring you out."

That seemed likely. Flesh and blood could only stand so much, and when men and women had seen their neighbors dragged off in the middle of the night—well, what had happened was more or less inevitable.

"What about the other routes?"

"I think we would do well to rule out both Red and Gold," said Goron. "They both run through the same province as Green, and I would recommend against going anywhere near it at the moment. We have a reliable report that two Russland rifle divisions have moved into the province."

Two rifle divisions was enough to comb the province town by town and practically house by house. It meant somebody fairly high up in the Red Flame command was giving the orders.

It also meant two fewer rifle divisions the Eighth Army would be facing on the Gallic front. Fine. But that would not be much help to Blade and Rilla if they were caught, tortured, and shot while trying to make their way through those two divisions!

"All right. We'll cancel Red and Gold too. That leaves only Purple. Is it your recommendation?"

"Yes. We have also had to develop a new variation for Route Purple. This has not been transmitted to Englor, so you would not know of it."

"When will I learn it?" said Blade.

"You and Rilla will still make your rendezvous with the escort at one of three established pickups—either nineteen, twenty-two, or twenty-nine. Twenty-two is prime, the others are backups. You will be briefed on Route Purple Two when you have met your escort."

"I see," said Blade. The local underground was imposing its own more rigorous standards of security. There would be mutterings in Englor when word of this got back there. But the local people were in the right. They knew better what were the dangers and what were the necessary precautions. A route that Special Operations HQ did not know was a route that no spy there could expose. A route that Blade himself did not know was a route he could not reveal under torture.

Of course this could make things awkward for Blade and Rilla. If they missed all three of the pickup points, they would have no way of learning how to get to the new extraction point at the far end of Route Purple Two. On the other hand, if all three pickup points were out, it would almost certainly mean the Red Flames had moved in. There would be no Route Purple left. Then the most likely route out of Rodzmania for Blade and Rilla would be through the poison capsules Blade carried in his pack.

"All right," said Blade. It wasn't completely satisfactory, but then people who liked completely satisfactory solutions didn't often go into espionage work. "We'll use Route Purple Two."

Chapter 13

Richard Blade lay on his stomach under a bush. He wore Russland Ground Forces camouflage battledress with the insignia of a Senior Sergeant in the Security Forces. He carried a Degorov automatic pistol in an imitation-leather shoulder holster. In fact, everything on his body was standard Russland issue. No one looking at him would be able to tell that he was not what he seemed.

The only unusual item of equipment was the pair of binoculars Blade held to his eyes. They were a compact pair, magnifying six times and including a range finder and an infrared attachment. They were rather more sophisticated than anything the Red Flames had. Anyone examining them closely would quickly realize that Blade was certainly not what he seemed.

Nobody was likely to try to make that close examination. Here in Rodzmania, even a private of the Russland Security Forces was a figure to inspire terror or at least discourage casual curiosity. Even senior officers of the Security Administration frequently carried out important missions disguised as junior officers, civil servants, or NCOs. Not even regular Russland military personnel were likely to ask embarrassing questions of men in Security insignia.

So Blade was confident of his chances of moving around freely and safely. Of course he might meet some real Security troops. That was always possible in any land where the Red Flames ruled. But the nearest large Security bases were on the Russland border sixty miles away in one direction, and in the town of Karbo ninety miles away in another. Here in the resort country it would be very bad luck to meet anything more formidable than Ground Forces men on leave or local Rodzmanian constables, who would not be willing to have anything at all to do with any Russlander if they could possibly help it.

There was one other danger. A Security man wandering around alone might be a tempting victim for someone who hated the Russlanders beyond reason. The Red Flames had ruled in Rodzmania for more than a generation, and in that time they had given literally hundreds of thousands of people cause to hate them with a terrible passion. The Russlanders took terrible vengeance for any attacks on their men, but there were certain to be people careless of possible consequences. It would be ironic for Blade to be picked off by some demented Rodzmanian patriot, but it would be just as final as any other death.

Blade found a stone digging into his ribs. He shifted position, pried it loose, pushed it to one side, then went back to watching the lakeshore in front of him.

He would not have needed the binoculars merely to watch for Rilla Haran. If she came today, she would come down to the little gravel beach just below the wooded bluff where Blade lay in hiding. He wanted to make sure that no one else was coming along with Rilla. The geneticist's habit of coming down to this secluded cove to swim and sunbathe was well known. It was unlikely that anyone would suddenly become curious or suspicious about it, but Blade was taking no chances.

He stared out from under the bush at the green forests, the silver blue water of the lake, and the grayish white gravel on the beach. They stared back at him. The water rippled and the branches swayed under a gentle breeze. Nothing else moved in the water, on the land, or in the air above them.

The sun crept up in the sky and grew warm. It might have become uncomfortably hot and airless in the close-grown forest where Blade lay hidden. Fortunately, enough of the breeze off the lake trickled in under the bushes to make Blade's wait almost comfortable.

Blade's journey to the lake had been simple enough, since he was disguised as one of the crew of a big logging truck. At least it would have seemed simple to the average man. Blade knew how much organization and planning had gone into making his journey so simple. He also knew far too well how much danger there had been at each moment of the two days—danger to himself, but even more danger to all those in the underground who had done their work so well.

Suppose his forged identity papers hadn't stood up to inspection? Suppose some Russlander had decided to scan the truck's load, log by log, with a metal detector? Blade's gear and far too much else that was fatally compromising lay concealed snugly inside a hollow log at the bottom of the load. Of course a bomb also lay there, powerful enough to clear half a city block if incautious hands started working on the log. Blade knew there was much to be said for a quick death, especially when one considered what the Red Flames might do otherwise. There was even more to be said for a long life. It had been a relief to reach the end of the journey, climb down from the truck, pull on his gear, and vanish into the woods for the last leg of his journey.

Now he was here, waiting for his first rendezvous with Rilla Haran. She did not know when he would be meeting her, but she did know where and she did know a basic recognition code. That was all the underground had been able to get to her at the resort, but it should be enough for today. They could talk for however long it took to arrange the details of the next rendezvous, when Rilla would slip out of her cottage by night to meet Blade in the forest. After that would come the journey to one of the pickup points for Route Purple Two, the journey along that route, and at last the trip back to Englor.

Blade had just finished this mental summary when he saw movement between two trees just above the beach. He swung the binoculars for a closer look, pressing the focusing adjustment. The trees sprang out sharply, and so did the tall woman standing between them, looking out at the lake. For a moment she was half lost in the forest shadows, so that Blade could not recognize her. Then she came down the slope toward the beach, moving with a powerful but graceful stride. The sunlight caught her dark red hair so that it seemed to glow. Now Blade had no trouble at all in recognizing the woman he sought.

Rilla Haran would have looked like a stocky peasant

girl if she'd been any shorter than her actual five feet ten. As it was, her broad-boned, well-fleshed body had a regal quality, particularly when she moved. There was nothing dainty or fragile about her—she was lushly, impressively female. The brilliance and the skill she showed in her work seemed to be reflected in the perfection of her body and the grace of her movements.

Blade hoped his judgement of her was correct. Ever since he'd learned he was bringing out a woman, he'd hoped she was the sort who could hold her own on any journey or in any fight. Rilla Haran certainly looked like a woman who could react intelligently and handle herself well in a wide range of situations outside her laboratory.

Blade pulled a small signal light out of one pocket and clipped it to the binoculars. The light was activated by the same switch that controlled the infrared viewer, and threw a tightly focused beam of light wherever Blade looked. At night it was difficult and by day it was almost impossible for anyone not directly in line with the beam to see it. It was one of the handiest devices for field signaling that Blade had ever used.

As he finished clipping the signal light in place, Rilla reached the water's edge. She wore baggy brown slacks, a dark blue blouse, and sandals. She carried a ragged gray blanket and a green sweater folded over one arm, and a small canteen slung on one hip.

She kicked off her sandals with two neat jerks of her long legs, spread the blanket on the gravel, and put the sweater on top of it. She walked down for a few more steps, until the chill clear waters of the lake washed around her ankles. An almost blissful smile crossed her round, freckled face, making it look even more cheerful than before. Then she stepped back up onto the dry gravel and began stripping off her clothes.

She undressed so swiftly that to Blade she seemed to go from fully clothed to totally nude in a moment. The last thing she did was to undo the ribbon that held up her hair. Unbound, her hair flowed down over her shoulders and halfway down her back. It did not conceal the fine lines of her neck, the faint dusting of freckles on the evenly tanned skin of her shoulders, or the magnificent breasts that swelled so superbly. On a woman with smaller bones, those breasts would have made her seem almost top-heavy. On Rilla Haran they were perfectly in proportion, part of her robust beauty. Blade found himself wondering how all this solid, well-shaped flesh would feel in his arms.

Now Rilla threw her head back and raised her arms toward the sky, as if she were worshiping the sun. She bent backward with a grace that would have made an ugly woman seem sensuously desirable. It made Rilla Haran positively breathtaking. Her skin held the same even tan and light dusting of freckles all over. Some of the hair in the dark bush cradled between her round thighs had been bleached to a lighter shade by the sun. That subtle highlight somehow added still more to the erotic effect.

Blade carefully put aside all the sensuous visions that kept chasing one another through his mind. He raised the binoculars again, aimed them at Rilla, and pressed the switch for the signal light. He wanted to make contact as fast as possible, before the woman got too relaxed and lazy in the sun to be alert or before any unwanted visitors showed up.

The light flicked on. Blade watched Rilla, saw a little circle of light appear on her left breast, and raised the binoculars until he saw the light flicker across her face. She blinked and started to back out of the beam. Then Blade could almost see memory awaken in her. She stopped in mid-stride and stood motionless, her arms dropping to her sides, her eyes very wide, and her lips drawn into a tight, pale line.

He had her attention now. Blade began pressing the switch to transmit the letters of the recognition code. Each letter was a sequence of dots and dashes.

B—U—K—E

—and then the numbers:

1—5—9—7

Blade went through the sequence twice. He was starting it a third time when Rilla suddenly raised her hands and pressed both palms against the sides of her neck. That was the acknowledgment signal. Then she began to reply with the agreed-upon sequence of hand signals, keeping her hands in front of her body so that Blade and no one else could see their movements.

She went through her reply twice. Then she made the signal—hands folded across the stomach—that there was more to come. After that she pointed along the southern edge of the cove, clenched her fist twice, and repeated that sequence as well. Blade flashed the code for "acknowledged and understood," then put the binoculars away. Rilla stepped into the water, waded out until it was up to her waist, then plunged forward.

Blade sprang to his feet, picked up his gear, and began to move, keeping Rilla in sight as much as possible. Sometimes trees or bushes cut off his view of her, but each time he saw her again she was still swimming strongly. Her steady movements gave him the impression she could go on swimming like that for hours or even the whole day if she had to.

At last Blade broke out into the open and saw what must have been Rilla's intended rendezvous just ahead of him. A spur of bare gray rock curved out into the lake from the shore. Rilla was swimming strongly for the sheltered patch of water between the spur and the shore. There she and Blade would be completely invisible. No one watching from any other part of the cove would see anything more suspicious than Rilla swimming along the shore, disappearing briefly, then swimming back the way she came.

Blade crawled forward on his hands and knees, taking advantage of every rock, bush, and fold in the ground. He reached the water's edge to find the surface before him blank and empty. He was just beginning to worry about this when Rilla's water-sleek head popped up from the surface like a seal's.

She grinned. "It is good to know that you are real. I was beginning to wonder." The grin faded. "It is not a good situation at the resort." Her English was almost unaccented, but so precise that no one would mistake her for a native speaker.

"How is it not good?" said Blade.

"They have six uniformed Security men in since three days ago, instead of only two."

That was not as bad as Blade had feared. Six Security men—one section—could not do a very good job of covering a resort area that spread over a mile of shore and several miles of forest. On the other hand, there was no way to know how many more Security people had come in disguised as dishwashers, masseurs, or truck drivers.

"Do they seem to be investigating anything in particular? Or are they just wandering around waiting for something to turn up?"

Rilla took so long to answer that question that Blade began to wonder if she hadn't understood. When she did answer, he realized she'd merely been trying to give as precise an answer as she could. Nude, treading the cold waters of the lake, and confronting an Imperial secret agent, she was still determined to give a scientist's precise answer to any question. Blade's respect for her went up another notch.

"They go nowhere in particular," she said. "They have not spent enough time in any one place to see very much." She frowned. "I am almost certain they do not suspect me, yet."

"Good," said Blade. "Can you be ready to escape tonight?"

"Tonight?"

"If you can, take what you'll need," Blade added.

She nodded. "I have the essential material of my research on film, everything that is not common knowledge. I have no hiking gear, though. I do not think it would be wise for me to try to get it."

She was probably right. "Do you at least have good shoes? That's the one thing you're certain to need. We've got at least a twenty-five-mile walk ahead of us, possibly twice that much."

Another nod. "Oh yes, I have that. It will not be hard for me to get out of my cottage at night, either. Where do I meet you?"

Blade disliked the idea of using the same place twice. On the other hand, where they were now offered the best concealment of any place along the whole shore of the cove. Anywhere else, even a casual passerby might catch a glimpse of them. Security men were close at hand, so that casual passerby might feel more willing than usual to tell them what he'd seen, to prove his loyalty to the Red Flames.

Blade made a gesture that took in the water and the land around them. "Here, at midnight or as soon after that as you can come. Dress as warmly as you can, and try to bring some food."

Rilla smiled. It was obvious that she would have laughed out loud if there'd been no danger of being overheard. "My friend, I grew up in the North Country of Russland. There the woods stretch for ten days' fast walking from one village to another, and it does not go above freezing from September to May. Give me advice about things I do not know so well as traveling in forests."

Blade smiled back. "When the time comes, I will." He gave her the recognition code for the night rendezvous, then lay still while she swam back out into the cove and back toward the beach. Again she swam with a strong and sturdy grace of movement. Blade was half tempted to wait and watch her climb out of the water again. He would not at all mind seeing her body gleaming naked in the sun again.

But it was never wise to spend a single unnecessary second in any place that might be dangerous. Before Rilla was halfway to the beach Blade was crawling back up the slope again. Long before she climbed out of the water he was back in the forest, heading for his hiding place and the few hours of sleep he would need before the night's work began.

Chapter 14

Blade returned to the cove that night, grimly prepared to have any number of things go wrong. Much to his surprise and delight, nothing at all out of the ordinary happened.

He reached the shore at 11:30 and lay under cover in the forest until midnight. Then he crawled along the shore and out onto the little rock spur, far enough to be well hidden. Then he lay down again to wait. Half of any field mission was always waiting for things to happen, to him or to others.

Rilla Haran came slipping along the shore just before one o'clock in the morning. A half-moon gave Blade enough light to see her clearly without the infrared viewer. She was carrying a small sack over one shoulder and a walking stick cut from a fallen branch in one hand. She was also quite obviously having to work hard to keep her nerves under control.

Blade didn't blame her. Her long training and brilliant scientific mind were no real preparation for tonight or anything that might come after tonight. Before tonight she'd been in comparatively little danger. The Security Administration might suspect her, but scientists like her were seldom bothered without very good reason. They were too valuable to the Red Flames' war effort.

After tonight, though, Security would have all the reasons they could need to arrest her, torture her, and stand her up against a wall. She had made her final break with the Red Flames. After tonight she would be out in the open, exposed, vulnerable, and protected only by men whose abilities she had no way of knowing. This would last until she reached Englor.

So Rilla had plenty of reasons to be even more nervous than she seemed.

At the edge of the forest she stopped, crouched down, and gave the recognition signal three times. Then she slid back under a bush, waiting and watching. Blade crept out of cover and returned her signal. Then he crawled along the shore until he was safely hidden behind the same clump of bushes that sheltered Rilla.

"Any trouble?" he whispered.

She shook her head, licked dry lips, and swallowed several times. Then suddenly she raised her head and kissed him lightly on the cheek. "Thank you," she said quietly.

Blade smiled. "Wait until you've got a little more to be thankful for. We've got a bit of a way to go yet."

They moved out through the forest at a good pace, one neither of them would have any trouble keeping up for days on end. If they did end up having to walk for days, it would mean something had gone fatally wrong with Route Purple Two, and they would have very little chance of getting out of Rodzmania alive. Blade was also determined that even if things came to that they would still go down fighting, and that meant saving their strength.

They covered half the distance to the primary pickup before dawn. They could have gone farther, but ahead lay a stretch of farming country with fewer woods to provide cover. They found shelter in the cellar of an abandoned farmhouse and settled down for the day, taking alternate three-hour watches. The day passed without trouble and with few signs that there were any other human beings in all the world. Blade found he could easily imagine he and Rilla were Adam and Eve, alone in a world just created out of whatever had gone before it.

If this was Eden, though, it held far too many snakes, in the form of Russland soldiers.

At nightfall they moved on. They had to move more carefully during this night's march, giving the scattered farms a wide berth, staying off the roads, and twice ducking for cover as Russland patrols passed too close for comfort. One patrol was eight soldiers in two jeeplike vehicles, the other was a truck bristling with machine guns and searchlights, which fortunately weren't turned on.

Two patrols were nothing unusual. No doubt the Red Flames had discovered Rilla's disappearance by now. But they didn't seem to have launched an all-out manhunt. Even when they did, it might not be disastrous. They might indeed comb the land house by house, but that would take time—perhaps more than enough time for Blade and Rilla to make their way safely along Route Purple Two and home to Englor.

They were only four miles from the pickup at dawn. Again they found safe cover while the sky was still gray and settled down as comfortably as they could. This day's cover was under a bridge, a damp hiding place swarming with mosquitoes that kept both of them from getting any sleep. Rilla was bitten until her eyes were swollen half shut, but she did not protest.

"Mosquitoes are nothing," she said, brushing some off her neck. "To get away from my masters, I think I would risk tigers or sharks. The Red Flames give a scientist much, so it was easy to do what they wanted for a long time. Too easy, and too long, I think. I was not as strong as I should have been, not soon enough." She shook her head. "They asked what they should not have, and I gave them more than I should have. Now it is too late for me, but perhaps for others, there is still time."

Blade didn't know what to make of these rather cryptic words, and didn't particularly care for their grim, almost fatalistic tone. He did not try to get anything more out of Rilla about her work.

Then the day ended and they started out across the last four miles. Blade would not have been at all surprised if the pickup point had been deserted, perhaps with some coded sign that it had been permanently abandoned. He was even prepared to find nothing at all, or even several bodies littering the grass and a Russland machine gun trained on them from the woods.

Instead he found four men who gave the proper recognition signals and understood his. That was exactly as he'd expected. What he hadn't expected was that one of the four men would be Piedar Goron. By now they were well outside Goron's normal area of operation, the area he knew as well as he might know the face of his wife. Blade had thought Goron was too good an underground man to take the risks involved in moving outside his own territory, except in an emergency.

Goron took Blade aside as soon as they'd moved a safe distance into the forest. "There is going to be a problem in getting you and Rilla out of here, one we had not anticipated."

"Purple Two's blown?"

Goron shook his head. "I wish it were that simple. No, as far as we know, it is still secure. Or it would be, if we could use it."

"Why can't we use it?"

"They will not let us."

"*Who* won't let us?" Blade's irritation showed in his voice. Goron seemed to want to talk in riddles, and Blade was in no mood to put up with it. Or had something happened to shake Goron so badly that he couldn't speak clearly and concisely?

With a little prompting from Blade the story came out. It was quite simple. A Priority One message had come to the Rodzmanian underground from Englor. It had stated that no, repeat *no,* deviations from any of the standard routes were to be used in connection with Operation Housepainter—Rilla Haran's defection.

"A flat prohibition?" said Blade.

"Yes."

"No reason given in the message?"

"None." That didn't sound like R. Blade was almost certain enough of that to say it out loud, but not quite. Damn it, he wished he knew just a little bit more than he did about the ways and methods of the Special Operations Division, enough to know whether R ever sent messages like this one. He would have known that much if he'd really been a senior Special Operations man, with fifteen years' experience as an Independent. But he was Richard Blade, stranger from another Dimension. He knew enough about Special Operations to do a competent job for it in the field, but not enough to guess what might go on in the Division's bureaucracy at home.

Unfortunately, there was no reason why someone in Englor could not have given this half-witted order. An intelligence organization could easily commit all the errors, crimes, and follies of any other bureaucracy, and a few more besides.

"The message had the standard double confirmation?" said Blade, probing further.

"Yes, damn it!" exploded Goron. His anger burst out in a roar that made birds and small animals dart away in fright. It seemed loud enough to be heard beyond the edge of the forest, a good three miles away.

Blade decided to let the issue drop. Further questioning would not alter the facts or produce any essential or even useful information. It would simply add to the strain that Piedar Goron was already enduring, and Blade would do much to avoid that. He would do nothing to add to the burdens of Goron and his comrades in the Rodzmanian underground.

Goron seemed to sense this change in Blade. He took several deep breaths, and when he spoke again his voice was level and calm. "We will still use Route Purple Two, but we will use the same exit as Purple One. That should keep them happy in Englor. There is no critical increase in risk. In fact, conditions are unusually favorable for the exit operation. Number 37's squadron is on a field-deployment exercise, so—"

The plan unfolded, Blade's mind worked along two parallel tracks, assessing the plan as he memorized it. It seemed entirely acceptable. It would certainly get Rilla and him back to Englor days or even weeks faster than any other plan, if it worked as Goron described it.

And if it didn't? Well, if it didn't, Blade and Rilla would at least be near the seacoast, and the sea still belonged to Englor. Once again there was a road home across the sea, if all else failed.

Chapter 15

The edge of a fog bank lay across the airfield, creeping in from the sea only five miles away. It made the darkness even deeper, dimming the runway lights to faint and fuzzy yellow glowworms somewhere far off in an unguessable distance.

Blade rolled down the window of the truck cab and peered out into the darkness. From the map and what he'd seen before the fog closed in, Blade could reconstruct everything within two miles of where the truck was parked.

In front of the truck lay the concrete strip of the runway, stretching half a mile off to the left and a mile to the right. On the far side of the runway was a parking strip. On it stood a dozen light bombers of the Sixth Maritime Patrol Squadron of the Rodzmanian Air Force. One of those bombers would take Rilla and Blade home across the Nord Sea to Englor.

Of course they would need some help. Blade looked past Piedar Goron at the wheel of the truck and off to the left, to see if that help could be in sight yet. There was nothing to see except the dim lights of the airfield's hangars and control tower. Blade looked at his watch and realized that it was still a good ten minutes before the pilot was due.

"Thank God, Josip is in a maritime squadron," said Goron. "Otherwise we would not be able to do our work tonight. The regular bomber squadrons do not fly in this kind of weather. There are not many Rodzmanians in the maritime squadrons, either, and most of those are truly faithful to the Red Flames." Goron's face twisted, as if he wanted to spit at that thought.

The pilot that Blade knew only as Josip came from an old and distinguished Rodzmanian family. In this respect he was unlike most Rodzmanians who had been permitted to join the armed forces under Red Flame rule. Most of them were "the people from nowhere," as Goron put it. They were fervently loyal, and any of them would gladly shoot Blade, Rilla, Goron, and Josip without thinking twice.

Josip was different. He came from among those Rodzmanians who normally held themselves rigidly aloof from the Red Flames. So when he wanted to serve them, they welcomed him with open arms. At thirty he was a lieutenant colonel in the Rodzmanian Air Force, with power and privileges superior to nearly all Rodzmanians and a good many Russlanders as well.

He'd paid a price for this, of course. Not all the Russlanders trusted or accepted him, and his own people despised him. His family not only never spoke to him, they never spoke of him. Even by the standards of the underground, his life was a lonely and grim one. Blade was glad Josip would be flying them out to Englor, to enter a life of exile but also of freedom—freedom to work openly against Russland, more freedom than any Rodzmanian could hope to know until the Red Flames were driven out.

Blade turned to look into the back of the truck where Rilla sat cross-legged on a pile of toolboxes and empty ammunition crates. She wore the same clothes she'd worn away from the resort, and over them a winter flying jacket so bulky that it almost concealed even her spectacular figure. She was pale and silent, obviously very much on edge but just as obviously doing a heroic job of concealing it. Blade was tempted to try giving her some reassurance, but decided against it. She was proud enough to resent it.

Blade also didn't want to try filling her with an assurance he didn't feel himself. Perhaps it was just the darkness and the fog, but his intuition told him that this affair was not going to run smoothly right to the end. He wanted very badly to believe that by dawn they would be drinking strong tea and eating eggs and bacon in Englor. He couldn't quite manage it.

The minutes crept by and the fog thickened. The world outside seemed as if it had always been dark and silent and always would be. Then Goron stiffened, and his indrawn breath hissed between his teeth. Blade saw it too. A faint blue white glow was growing in the fog far away to the left. Slowly it turned into a pair of headlights, and behind the headlights appeared the hood and windshield of a staff car.

Blade turned to signal Rilla to lie down on the floor, but she was already doing it. Her breath was coming fast and hard, as if she'd been running. Blade opened the door on his side and climbed out. Goron did the same. Blade unzipped his jacket and unsnapped the shoulder holster that held the little automatic. It had no silencer, but the cartridges were specially stepped-down, useless at twenty feet but deadly at five, and practically noiseless.

The staff car came on fast. For a moment Blade wondered if Josip was going to be able to stop it in the right place. Then the brakes squeaked faintly and the car pulled to a stop, skidding slightly on the wet concrete. The man called Josip opened the right-hand front door and climbed out, his face showing polite surprise.

"What's the trouble?" he said briskly.

That was the signal for action. Blade put both hands on the right front fender, vaulted clear over the hood, and landed on the far side of the car. With one hand he jerked open the driver's door and with the other he drew the automatic and fired two rounds squarely into the driver's face. The stepped-down cartridges made only faint popping noises. The driver made no noise at all as he slid out of the seat and landed on his back on the runway.

At the same moment, one of Josip's crewmen opened the rear door on the far side and tried to scramble out. He was just straightening up when Goron closed in, caught the man by the hair with one hand, and with the other drove a knife up under his chin.

The other crewman got out of the car before Blade could move against him, but no farther. Blade wheeled on one foot and drove the other into the man's groin. He doubled up. Before he could fall Blade grabbed him by the collar of his flying suit, jerked him forward, and chopped the other hand down across the back of the man's neck with lethal force.

Three men down, no noise anyone could have heard more than ten feet away, no radio calls, and no visible damage to the staff car. A good job, carried out from start to finish in less than thirty seconds.

Blade picked up the body of the second crewman and carried it to the truck. Goron did the same with the body of his victim. Josip pushed the driver in on top of the other two bodies, then climbed in himself.

Goron started the truck off again, following Josip's directions. The pilot's face was as gray as the fog outside and wet with either fog or sweat or both. "I've drawn Six Nine Six," he said quietly. "Rules for bad-weather operations call for a maximum fuel load. We have plenty to take us to Englor, even at low altitude, and no one suspects anything."

The truck pulled to a stop by one wing of the patrol bomber. Josip slid out of the back, Blade and Rilla followed him, and Goron climbed out of the driver's seat to join the others. Blade held a machine pistol taken from one of the dead crewmen and three hand grenades dangled from his belt.

The patrol bomber loomed above them, looking lean and rakish even in the darkness and the fog. An aluminum ladder was propped against the left wing. Josip went over to the ladder and began to climb.

"I must radio in that I am at the plane," he said.

"Can't you wait until we've started the engines?" said Blade. "Then we can move fast if we have to."

Josip shook his head. "Then they would be suspicious. I am sorry, but there is no other way. When I have made the call, I will open the belly hatch for you and the woman."

"I'll climb up on top," said Blade. "I think one of us had better keep watch until you've started the engines and Piedar is out of sight."

Goron turned so that he could reach out with one hand to Blade and with the other to Rilla. "I would like to see you people take off, of course, but—"

"You realize that it's time you were on your way," Blade finished for him.

Goron laughed. "Yes, I suppose so. I suppose I should not even have come this far, but I could not do otherwise. Not after that many-times damned order from Englor."

Blade said nothing, for there was nothing to say about that order that he hadn't already said several times. He would cheerfully strangle whoever gave it with his bare hands, but that would have to wait until he was back in Englor.

Blade scrambled up the ladder, feeling it creak under his weight, and climbed onto the wing. The dull gray aluminum was slick underfoot, and he moved carefully as he made his way toward the fuselage.

Blade reached the fuselage and looked forward. Josip was already in the cockpit, head bent over the controls. The whirr of a starter floated up to Blade's ears, and the truck with Piedar Goron at the wheel jerked into motion.

Blade raised one hand in a silent salute to the underground leader. He would have given a good part of his own chances at a safe return to Englor to get Goron safely out of here.

It happened so fast that if Blade's own intuition hadn't already made him partly alert, even his own swift and skilled reactions might not have been enough. A sudden *crack* overhead, like the blast of a shotgun, and the fog and the wet concrete and the aluminum of the plane seemed to glow as a flare burst high above the runway. Even in the fog it blazed so fiercely that for a moment Blade did not see the headlights racing toward him down the runway. He could only hear the swelling roar of engines, but that was enough to finish alerting him. By the time he could see clearly again, he knew where to look for the enemy.

There were three vehicles racing toward him. In the lead was a small jeep with three men in civilian clothes in it. Behind the jeep was a large canvas-topped truck. In the rear was an armored car, the commander standing up in the turret and the driver visible in the front hatch.

Blade's arm curved and his hand closed on one of the grenades. In a single flowing motion he jerked the pin, swung his arm far back, and snapped it forward. The grenade arched through the fog. As the flare died it struck the runway only a few feet ahead of the jeep. At the exact moment the jeep passed above it, the grenade exploded.

The blast lifted the jeep completely clear of the ground and in the same moment ignited the gas tank in a searing flash of yellow white flame. The sound of screaming men and crumpling metal as the jeep fell back to the ground were lost in the roar of the flames.

With a desperate twist of the wheel, the driver of the truck avoided ramming the flaming wreckage of the jeep. As the truck swerved, one tire must have passed over some sharp fragment of metal. There was another shotgun sound as the tire blew and a squeal of rubber as the truck went into a wild skid. It swung left, the driver fighting desperately for control, as the men in the back started leaping for safety. Three came out, two going down and not rising, a third staggering to his feet with his rifle still in his hands. Blade started to pull the pin from another grenade, then suddenly realized where the truck was going to end up. Instead, he leaped down from the plane's fuselage onto the wing, no longer worrying about slipping on the wet metal.

He was still fighting for balance on the wing when the skidding truck crashed into the plane. The truck tore off the nose landing gear and the nose smashed down onto the truck's cab. Blade lost his footing and nearly skidded right off the trailing edge of the wing. For a moment he had the feeling that the plane was going to flip right over like a playing card and land with him underneath.

Blade flung himself on his belly toward the leading edge of the wing, raising his machine pistol as he did. This was the kind of close fighting where it was deadly. A single burst emptied the magazine and cut down four Russland soldiers as they struggled out of the truck.

Blade threw his second grenade, aiming for a tear in the canvas top of the truck. His throw was good. Fragments of metal, canvas, human bodies, and weapons showered down all around. The truck's gas tank spewed flame. Blade took advantage of the moment's confusion to swing himself over the edge of the wing. He hung by his hands for a moment, then dropped to the concrete.

As he put a new magazine in the machine pistol, the cockpit canopy opened and Josip scrambled out onto the fuselage. His face was set and grim, and he carried a pistol in his right hand. At that moment Blade saw that the armored car was stopped out on the runway and the machine gun in the turret was swinging toward the plane. Josip straightened up, Blade yelled a warning, and the machine gun gave a quick, angry rattle. Josip's uniform turned dark from chest down to groin and his face set even harder. He reeled, fired two shots from his pistol, and toppled off the plane.

As Josip struck the concrete, Rilla ran out from where she'd been waiting under the plane. Blade shouted to her, "Get down!" and practically dragged her to the concrete with him. He shifted the machine pistol to a two-handed grip and sighted in on the armored car's commander in his turret.

Then the turret began to swing again and Blade saw something move in toward the armored car from the edge of the parking area. It was Piedar Goron in his truck, turning his back on the safety he might have found in the forest to come back and try to salvage a mission gone spectacularly wrong. The machine gun went off, and at the same time Goron fired out his window. He had a poor angle and a moving platform, but his submachine gun didn't need precise aiming. A long burst filled the air around the armored car with bullets. The commander crumpled in his hatch and the turret stopped turning as his body jammed it. Goron's truck screeched to a stop, and Blade leaped to his feet. He dashed out into the open, avoiding bodies and nearly slipping on concrete now slippery with blood and leaking fuel from the plane. He ran up to the driver's hatch of the armored car and put a burst from his machine pistol into the chest of the man inside.

As Blade reached in to pull the driver out of the car, Goron came stumbling up. He limped, one arm dangled uselessly, there was blood in the corner of his mouth and a long ugly bullet graze along one cheek. He was obviously hurt, probably badly.

Rilla ran out to join them as Blade pulled the dead commander out of the turret. The paleness of her face was now broken by several large smudges of grease or soot, and her hands shook slightly. But she was enough in control of herself to help Goron into the car. Blade finished with the commander, took the man's pistol and gloves, and climbed into the car. He gave a desperate mental prayer for it to start and nearly shouted out loud in relief and delight as the engine rumbled into life. Then he swung the car around to pass close to the plane.

Goron bit back a gasp of pain and stared at Blade. "Why—this?"

"Confuse our trail a bit," said Blade. Without stopping he took one hand off the wheel to pick up his last grenade. He pulled the pin with his teeth, then heaved the grenade out the window and up onto the wing of the plane. As it exploded, he slammed one size twelve shoe down on the gas pedal. The armored car swerved wildly, started to skid, straightened out, and roared away down the runway as the patrol bomber erupted in flames behind it.

Blade shifted gears and shouted to Rilla, "Keep a lookout behind!" He shifted gears again, and the hammering roar of the diesel under the hood grew louder. In the rearview mirror Blade could see the flames mounting higher and higher and spreading farther and farther as burning fuel flowed out across the runway. The Russlanders would undoubtedly want to come after them, but they'd also be worried about putting out the flames before they spread to other planes, reopening the runway, and—

Blade stared. Through the fog, high above the trees at the far end of the runway, he could see a set of lights, red and green and white, rapidly growing larger. Somehow the airfield hadn't suspended flight operations. Now a plane was coming in to land on the runway, possibly right on top of them.

The armored car shook as the burning plane's bomb load went off with a tremendous crash, sending the flames higher and scattering great chunks of metal in all directions. Blade pushed the gas pedal all the way to the floor and the car shot forward in a cloud of smoke and spray from the wet runway. Goron let out a gasp of pain as he was thrown back into his seat. Rilla was silent, biting her lip until Blade could see drops of blood on it.

Somewhere far behind them a machine gun opened up. Where it was shooting from and what it was shooting at, Blade didn't know or care, as long as it was out of range. Perhaps the gunners in their fright and confusion might shoot down the incoming plane before the control tower could guide it clear!

The machine gunners somehow managed to hold their fire in time. The incoming plane, a twin-engined transport, sailed in only yards above the armored car. It touched down smoothly five hundred feet behind the car, and also five hundred feet short of where wreckage and flames completely blocked the runway. Blade heard the shrill whine of turboprops thrown into reverse and a desperate squealing of tires as the pilot saw what lay ahead and frantically tried to stop his plane.

Blade saw the transport plane roll swiftly and with a deadly inevitability straight into the flames. He saw it shudder and slue wildly as tires blew. Miraculously, it did not flip over or break apart. It was still intact as it lurched to a stop squarely in the middle of the flames. There was a long moment when Blade saw doors flying open and small dark figures frantically leaping out. Then plane and leaping figures all vanished in a great swelling globe of flame as the fuel tanks went up. The rearview mirror showed more flaming fragments whirling through the air, to skip along the runway or slash into parked bombers. More flames roared up as two of the bombers caught fire.

Blade heard Rilla gasp and Goron put all his remaining strength into a feeble cheer. Then the end of the runway appeared ahead, sweeping rapidly toward them. Blade eased off on the gas. The car slowed slightly as it ran off the concrete and rumbled onto the grass beyond the end of the runway.

A hundred yards away the perimeter fence of the airbase took shape out of the fog. Blade saw barbed wire, a wooden gate with a tower flanking it, uniformed figures running frantically, the flash of rifles. He heard the *tang-ting-tonnnng* of bullets on the armor and a *crack* as the radio antennas were shot off. He heard no blasts of tires going flat or booms of fuel tanks igniting. He grinned savagely, aimed the car straight for the wooden gate, and jammed the accelerator to the floor again.

The massive forged double bumper and inch-thick frontal armor of the car drove through the wooden gate like an ax through an orange crate. Wood splintered and flew, wire parted with sharp twangs, the thick glass of the windshield cracked clean across but did not shatter inward. Churned-up gravel thundered against the car's belly as Blade turned it onto the access road; more bullets rattled on the side and rear armor.

Then they were away into the darkness and the fog, moving so fast that in a minute even the roaring flames on the airfield faded into the night. They raced on alone, the booming roar of the diesel making it impossible to talk and almost impossible to think. They roared on, with the night all around them, for all they could tell the only human beings left alive in all the world.

Eventually they came to a patch of woods at the bottom of a hill. At the top of the hill Blade could make out a sign and a short stretch of what looked like a paved highway. He pulled off the gravel road into the shelter of the trees and stopped the car.

Goron let out a long sigh, wincing with the pain it caused him. Then he spoke, his voice strained and low, with an ugly bubbling sound deep in his throat as he breathed.

"You should leave the car here. It will be harder for them to find you if you go on foot. I can stay here and fight them when they find the car."

Blade shook his head. "We'll do a damned sight better in the car. If I remember correctly, that road up there is National Highway 32. If we take it north for about sixty miles, we'll be in good territory for stealing a boat and heading offshore."

"A boat?" asked Rilla.

Blade controlled his reluctance to give out unnecessary information and nodded. "Yes. There's an uninhabited island off the coast that's regularly visited by Imperial submarines. If we can reach it and hold out for about ten days, I expect we will be picked up without any more trouble.

"If we go on foot, it will be three days before we can reach the fishing villages. If we stay with the car, we can be well out to sea before the fog lifts tomorrow morning. Also, there's Piedar. I don't see how he can travel on foot in his condition."

Goron stared at Blade. "But I do not—"

"We're not going to abandon you here, and stop trying to talk us into it. Is there any underground cell anywhere along Highway 32 where we could leave you?"

Reluctantly, Goron nodded.

"Good," said Blade. "Rilla, help him into the back and—you know first aid, I hope?"

"Yes."

"There's a kit in my pack. Make him as comfortable as possible and try to keep him warm. Then keep a lookout behind, though I think it will be a while before we're pursued. They were certainly expecting us at the airfield. But we've left a bit of a shambles behind us. I don't think they were expecting that. By the time they've counted what's left of the bodies and figured out who did what to whom, we can be well on our way."

"What about the guards at the gate?"

"They may be able to make a good guess which way we went," Blade admitted. "But—Rilla, you know how the Red Flames' forces work. You think they'll be coming after us without orders?"

Rilla managed a shaky smile, her first in hours. "No. I think you are right." She rose to her knees and reached around between the seats for Goron. "Come, friend Piedar. Come back here and try to sleep. I think this has gone on longer for you than for us."

Goron tried to speak but could only nod as he tried to lift himself out of the seat. He was halfway out of the seat when he gave a great choking cry, spraying blood from his nose and mouth all over the windshield, the dashboard, and Blade. Then he gave a fainter choke, more blood trickled from his mouth, and he fell back into the seat.

Blade lifted one limp arm and felt for the pulse. He felt it continue strongly for a few more seconds, then slowly fade away to nothing. He let go of the dead man's hand and wiped the blood off his own face. Then without a word he started the engine again, put the car into gear, and headed up the hill.

Chapter 16

Blade could never forget that wild ride through the night and the fog along Rodzmania's National Highway 32, with a dead man in the seat beside him and a white-faced woman crouching behind him. Of the many experiences of his adventurous life, it was certainly one he would have been glad to forget if he could.

He kept the gas pedal flat to the floor. He knew he did not speak, and he could not be sure he even breathed as the armored car roared north. From time to time he blessed the lack of initiative of the Red Flames' armed forces, and also the ruggedness and reliable engines of their armored cars. This type of armored car had a rated top speed of sixty miles an hour, according to the manuals. Blade didn't drop below seventy for the first half hour of the ride. The road was smooth and traffic didn't exist; he would have hit a hundred if the car could have done it.

After that first half hour he slowed down to an almost leisurely fifty. That was still fast enough to make them a difficult target in the misty darkness and carry them easily through all but the stoutest of roadblocks.

Blade would have been happier if the radio antennas hadn't been shot away. Then they might have been able to listen to the enemy's command network and find out how the hunt for them was developing. But as it was, there was nothing to do but push on and hope speed and boldness would keep luck on their side through the night.

It did. By two in the morning they were well into the area where small fishing villages studded the coves and bays along the shore. They pulled off Highway 32 onto a side road leading to a cliff overlooking the sea. Blade drove up the winding road while Rilla stood in the turret, her hair tossing in the breeze from the sea. The fog eddied erratically, now thicker than ever, now thinning out to the faintest mist.

They reached the top of the cliff at a moment when the fog was so thin they could look across several miles of open sea. For the first time that night they could even look up and see the stars.

Blade walked along the cliff until he found a place where the rim sloped downward, steepening gradually until it reached a vertical drop of two hundred feet to the sea below. He stripped the armored car of everything he and Rilla could use and carry, then strapped Piedar Goron's body into the passenger seat.

Slowly Blade drove the car to the top of the sloping

rim, turned it onto the slope, then flung the door open and sprang clear. He landed hard, rolled to break his fall, saw the swinging door flash over him. He sat up and watched as the car went rumbling down the slope, moving faster and faster, swaying wildly from side to side. Then it steadied, rolled the last few yards, and plunged out into empty air. Blade held his breath until the sound of the splash floated up from below. The maps showed water a hundred feet deep at the foot of the cliff. Their trail would be safely broken, and Piedar Goron would have a tomb safe from disturbance by the Red Flames.

When the last sounds of the splash died away, Blade walked down to where Rilla sat on a boulder and helped her to her feet. "It's time we went to find ourselves a boat," he said.

She nodded. "Will you tell me where the island is, and how the submarine will pick me up?"

"I thought you couldn't handle a boat?"

"Perhaps not. But fear is not a bad teacher, and my luck might last even if yours does not."

"And if yours doesn't last either?" said Blade quietly.

"Then I will find a clean death and a clean grave in the sea, like Piedar Goron's, not what the Red Flames will give me if they catch me."

Blade took her hand, and side by side they walked down the hill. As they walked, the fog again grew thick around them.

It was still thick at dawn, but by that time they were twenty miles out to sea.

Rilla's advice helped Blade choose a boat. In the first village, he would have chosen a heavily timbered cruiser with a full rig to supplement the engine. Rilla shook her head at that.

"I think that no one but a Red Flame or a collaborator would have such a boat here. If it is stolen, the owner will make a great cry. The local police and the Russland patrols will have to listen to him.

"If we steal a fishing boat, it will be different. The fisherman will not be happy, but he will think his boat was stolen by another fisherman, by the Red Flames, or by the underground.

"He will try to find and kill the fisherman himself. He will know that it is useless to complain when the Red Flames take his property. If the underground has taken the boat, then he will be happy to have aided them with no real danger to himself. So if we take a fishing boat I do not think we will be pursued."

"Let's look for a fishing boat, then," he said. As long as the boat would get them safely to Englor if necessary, he didn't much care what kind it was.

They found their boat in the second village, a forty-foot ketch with the masts set unusually far apart and a rusty one-cylinder gasoline engine. Blade hoped they wouldn't have to use the engine much—it looked more useful for anchoring the boat than for moving it. But the rigging and sails were in good condition.

Working silently in the darkness Blade set the mainsail, and the boat crept slowly out across the little harbor and into the channel to the sea. It seemed to take forever to tack down the channel, with Blade at the helm and Rilla keeping a lookout forward.

Once they were clear of the channel Blade turned to the engine. Rather to his surprise, it started. It also made a pounding roar like a badly tuned racing car running without a muffler. Blade wasn't sure he shouldn't turn it right off again before it brought every fisherman for ten miles up and down the coast out on their trail. But it was either the engine or wait until the breeze rose. Blade chose the engine.

He also sent Rilla below to get some sleep in the tiny cabin aft. He practically had to push her, although she was reeling with fatigue. Before she went, she threw her arms around him and kissed him three times—once on each cheek, once on the lips. Under the warmth of those kisses Blade sensed Rilla's relief and gratitude, and also unmistakable desire. It was a desire kept carefully under control for the moment—Rilla was a woman who would know when to think of love and when to think only of survival. But when the right moment came, that control would crumble. Blade knew that the right moment would come before they said good-bye, and he was glad of that. There was much more he wanted to know about this woman, and the pleasure and excitement of that superb body of hers was part of it.

Meanwhile, there was a sea voyage to take—a hundred miles to the island of Steyra if they were lucky, a thousand miles to Englor if they were not. Blade settled himself as comfortably as he could manage on the cracked and moldy cushions of the seat and clamped his hand firmly on the wheel.

Dawn crept through the clouds and the fog two hours after sunrise. By ten there was a faint hint of breeze. By the time Rilla awoke the fog was vanishing from around them, and a brisk wind was filling the mainsail. Blade showed Rilla the basic art of steering a boat under sail, then lay down on the cushions where he would be within easy call. His eyes were closed two minutes after he put his head down.

Chapter 17

They reached the island of Steyra at dawn the next morning. This dawn was sparkling bright, with the sky glowing as the sun crept up over the horizon and the breeze raised whitecaps on the sea. It was a lovely sight, and Blade was glad to be able to make the approach to the island with good visibility. Good visibility for him, though, meant the same for anyone who sailed by or flew overhead. He would not have greatly minded another day of fog.

The island of Steyra was twelve miles long and four miles wide. Because of its poor soil it was uninhabited. Parties of fishermen came from time to time to gather shellfish and seabirds' eggs, but that was all. Most of the island was rock, as bare and lifeless as an army helmet, but on both coasts there were a number of bays where a fair-sized boat could ride safely at anchor—or a submarine enter submerged. Three of the bays were regularly visited by Imperial submarines on patrol in these waters, and it was for one of those bays that Blade set his course.

They made their way close-hauled around to the western side of the island, reaching the mouth of the bay by noon.

Blade lowered the sails while Rilla took the wheel and steered them into the cove under power. By now she handled the boat as confidently as if she'd been doing it for years. The sea breeze and the release of tension had brought some color back to her bleached cheeks.

At last they came to a place half a mile inside the bay where they could moor directly to the rock. Blade sprang from the bow onto the shore and led the bowline around a handy boulder, while Rilla lowered the anchor from the stern.

Blade wiped his hands on his trousers and looked up. The cliffs around the bay rose a hundred feet high on all sides. No one but the seabirds wheeling high overhead could see them now. There was much else that would have to be done before they could safely settle down and wait for the submarine, but none of it had to be done in the next few hours. For the first time since he'd dropped from the Imperial reconnaissance plane into Rodzmania, Blade didn't feel a need to keep alert.

Rilla walked forward to the bow and stood by the bowsprit, smiling down at Blade. The cliffs all around cut off the sea breeze, and the damp air was almost warm. Rilla pulled off her jacket and threw it down on the deck. Then she took two steps out along the bowsprit and sprang lightly down onto the rock. Two more steps, and Blade found her coming into his arms, her eyes wide and her lips curved in a broad smile before they pressed themselves against his.

They had both known this would happen when the moment seemed right. Now that moment was here.

Blade felt desire roar up within him, as vivid and real as the burning planes on the airfield. He held Rilla against him, feeling her warmth, the lush magnificence of her body, the trembling that told of a desire that was rising in her to match his. Then he stepped away from her and laughed, although the laugh came strangely from his dry throat.

"For God's sake let's get something to spread on the rocks, or we're going to look like we've fallen off the cliffs by the time we're through."

"Ah," said Rilla, tossing her head so that her hair rippled across her shoulders. "You are right." She began to unbutton her sweater. "So go and get a sail or a blanket. Do not be slow."

Blade nodded and leaped back aboard the boat. It seemed that he went from bow to stern in two leaps, then dove below into the tiny cabin to snatch blankets from the narrow bunks. Back on deck, forward again—and he stopped at the foot of the bowsprit to stare and admire.

Rilla stood by the boulder to which the boat was moored, one hand resting on it, the other hand on her hip. All her clothes were tossed roughly over the boulder. She was as nude as she'd been by the cove on the lake, so many days and many miles ago. This time, though, she'd stripped to bare herself to far more than the sunlight and the wind and the water. The look in her eyes made that as clear as if she'd carved it into the rock at her feet. Those eyes were green, and they seemed far larger than before.

Blade did not remember passing from the boat to the shore. He did not remember taking off his own clothes, although he remembered Rilla telling him to do so in a choking voice. He did not remember sweeping the loose pebbles from a patch of rock and spreading the blankets out on it.

He could be sure that all of these things happened. He remembered very clearly how he lay down on the blankets and how Rilla stood above him. There was no urge to dominate in her; there was no desire to submit in him. There was only an overpowering sense that both of them wanted her to ride him and that it did not matter very much, because this joining would be only their first and not their last. They had all the time that even two people thrust forward by a fierce desire could possibly want or need.

Rilla bowed forward, and for a moment she saluted

with her lips the thickened rod of Blade's risen manhood. It was only a passing salute, and Blade was glad of that. There was only so much desire that any man's endurance could meet and conquer. The touch of Rilla's lips hinted at their ability to push his desire far beyond that point.

There would be time to test that ability, and much else about Rilla. That time was not now.

Rilla rose from her bow, balanced herself with her long, solidly curved legs spread wide apart, then lowered herself down upon Blade. He twisted upward to meet her and they joined, his thrust surging upward out of sight into the damp dark redness between her tanned thighs. A gasp broke through his lips, and on her face appeared a look not of fulfillment—that would come later—but of satisfaction that they were well and happily begun.

From that happy beginning they moved swiftly onward. She did not rise and fall, but instead writhed around and around and from side to side. Every part of the maddening warmth and the glorious wetness that surrounded Blade pressed against him. He had an exquisite sense of being caught and held in a grip that would never slacken or release him.

What Rilla felt he could only guess from the expressions that tumbled wildly across her face, as wildly as her hair tumbled about with each shake and twist of her head and body. Her eyes flickered open and shut and her nostrils flared wider and wider, as though she were running desperately and could not suck enough air into her panting lungs. Her teeth were clamped tightly shut, although her lips twisted into shapes that seemed to hold strange combinations of both pain and pleasure.

It could not go on this way for long, however determined Blade was to endure, however determined Rilla was to extract every bit of delight. She came to her first spasm, every part of her body jerking and twisting as though it would fly apart, her massive breasts with their solidly jutting nipples doing a strange, impassioned, infinitely provocative dance of their own. She came to a second spasm, and her head went back and a terrible and wonderful cry of release and fulfillment went echoing around the cliffs. She came to a third spasm—

—and this time Blade reached his own along with her. Two cries echoed around the cove, two bodies went through complex and totally uncontrolled movements, two sets of eyes clamped tightly shut, two pairs of hands sought each other and gripped until both cried out in pain as well as delight. Then there was silence and stillness, except for the heaving chests and the gasps as starved lungs tried desperately to suck in air. After a while even that faded away. Blade looked up at Rilla, Rilla looked down at Blade, and they both laughed.

"You know," he said at last. "I could stay here for hours. And so could you."

She nodded.

"But there are still things to do before we'll be safe."

She nodded again.

"So let's get ourselves up and do them!" He ran a hand lightly down her spine and slapped her smartly on the buttocks. Slowly and reluctantly she rose, and just as slowly and reluctantly he scrambled to his feet to join her.

They found a route up the cliffs and set up camp on top, overlooking the mouth of the bay. Concealed between two large boulders, the camp was sheltered both from the wind and from passing eyes. At the same time it gave them a much better view of all possible approaches to their refuge.

There would be little hope for them if anyone did come. If their presence on this bare and inhospitable island were known to an enemy, they would face a grim situation. Blade hoped Rilla did not realize how little hope there would be, although she had a surprising ability to calmly look great dangers and long odds in the face.

In any case, Blade's forebodings turned out to be unnecessary. If a hunt for them ever was launched, it certainly got nowhere near Steyra Island. They spent twelve days there, living on fish and on biscuit and salt meat from the fishing boat. They got a little hungry, but they still found the strength to make love every morning, almost every night, and sometimes at noon as well.

On their lucky thirteenth day an Imperial submarine appeared. On the eighteenth day after reaching Steyra Island they were safely back in Englor, and Rilla was able to report what the Red Flames were doing with her discoveries in genetics and cloning.

Unfortunately, no one would believe her.

Chapter 18

General Strong looked across his desk with an expression that seemed to indicate he wished the people facing him would vanish in a puff of smoke.

"Dragons?" he said.

Rilla nodded. "Dragons."

"Flying, fire-breathing dragons?"

She nodded again.

"Flying, fire-breathing dragons that are going to fly from the tops of the mountains of Nordsbergen and land in Englor?"

Rilla nodded a third time. "It would be more accurate to say that they will glide, General. They are too heavy to really fly, except in a very strong wind. But—"

Blade gently squeezed Rilla's hand and she fell silent. Blade did not much care for the tone in General Strong's voice. Granted that General Sir Morgan Strong was Director of the Office of Military Intelligence. That did not prove that he himself had any intelligence. Certainly he was showing very little of it now.

Blade felt like saying that aloud. On the other hand, Sir Morgan Strong was a full general. He himself was a major with a background that could not safely be subjected to close investigation. General Strong seemed like the type to investigate any major who talked out of turn.

Blade decided he would have to leave in R's hands the problem of coping with General Strong.

The one-eyed man took a deep breath. "General Strong, I assume you question the reliability of Miss

Haran's reports, in spite of her role in the creation of these dragons?"

General Strong obviously did. Just as obviously, he wasn't quite ready to come right out and call Rilla a high-priced defector, to her face and in R's presence. "Not altogether. It merely seems to me improbable, to the point that I am extremely reluctant to commit this office of His Imperial Majesty's Armed Forces to any course of action based on it."

R raised his bushy gray eyebrows, and Blade had the sense that battle had been joined. When R raised his eyebrows that way, it meant he'd made his decision. General Strong now had only two choices—he could surrender, or R would try to destroy him and probably succeed.

"You do not, I assume, question the existence of the cloning processes described in the material Miss Haran has presented?"

Again Strong shook his head. "No. I do not. I can say that definitely. I can also say that I see no logical reason why these processes should have been used to create—let us be frank, to create monsters out of children's fairy tales." This time it was Rilla who looked as if she wanted to speak bluntly to the general—or even breathe fire all over him, like one of her own dragons.

R nodded with elaborate politeness. Blade recognized that nod as one of satisfaction. General Strong now had plenty of rope to hang himself. "Then your decision is final, with regard to action on this report?"

"It is. As long as I hold this office, His Majesty's Armed Forces will not be diverted from action against their real enemies to guard against, still less pursue, fairy tales."

R chose to take those words as a dismissal. He gathered up Blade and Rilla with his eyes and they passed into the outer office.

Rilla's own bodyguards met them to escort her away. Blade took her aside into an alcove for a moment. Her arms went slowly around him, and her head rested on his shoulder.

"When they think it's safe, would you like to come

away on a private holiday with me for a few days? I imagine it could be arranged."

Rilla straightened up and looked at Blade. She was wearing high heels, and her eyes were nearly on a level with his. She looked at him in expressionless silence for a moment, then smiled.

"I would like that very much, Richard. I like the way you asked, too. It seemed you really wanted to know what I felt, and if I had said *no* you would have said nothing."

Blade smiled in his turn. "Don't get in the habit of crediting me with virtues I may not have."

"Ah, but that is one virtue you do have. You do not take me for granted. You are not the first man whose company I have found good, Richard. But you are the first who has not taken me for granted. I could care for you a great deal more than any of those other men, I think."

Blade felt like telling her that he was not a good man to care for, not with his duties and with the war so close. But she must already know that. If she was setting it all aside . . .

"Well," he said. "I think we can talk more of that some other time and place."

"And more than talk," she said, kissing him gently. She turned and walked out of the alcove to join her bodyguards.

When she'd gone, Blade and R went out to their staff car. As the car wound its way through London traffic toward the airport, R looked at Blade with a more than usually unreadable expression on his face and said quietly, "We have our evidence about Elva Thompson."

"Conclusive?"

"Eighty percent."

That was greater reliability than one could usually expect in intelligence matters. Whatever was about to happen to Elva would probably be well deserved.

A moment passed, and Blade realized that R seemed to be hesitating. That could hardly mean anything but bad news. Blade found himself resenting R's apparent notion that he was weak where Elva was concerned.

"Well?" he said abruptly.

"She is the center of Red Flame penetration of our Division. Not the only person involved, probably. But the key one."

Blade's head jerked. "Was she responsible for the fake order about not deviating from prescribed routes?"

"She was. That is good, in a way. It means we only need to eliminate a spy, instead of also searching for some dusty-brained idiot who gave that order in perfectly good faith. It was Elva. She'd been around long enough to know all our forms and procedures. It was easy enough for her to insert a false message into the proper channels and set you and—what was his name?"

"Piedar Goron."

"—up for that trap at the airfield. However, they set the trap for foxes. What they caught was a lion."

"Thank you, sir."

"Don't thank me. I should thank you for what you've done on this mission. You've got an absolutely matchless gift for this kind of work. I'll push it all the way up to the Minister of Defense if they don't approve you for lieutenant colonel at least."

"Yes, but what about Elva Thompson?"

"For the moment, she's where she can do us no further harm and the Red Flames no good. The Norfolk shadow headquarters is still just that. We're not proposing to give the shadow any real substance, either, not as long as she's there. When my estimate is that she's outlived all her usefulness, we'll have her killed. Make it look like an accident, you know. We don't want to tell the Red Flames any more than necessary about our internal security."

"Quite right," said Blade. He found it almost a relief that R—like J—could use the blunt, honest word "kill." Too many intelligence people were committed to euphemisms like "terminate." Both R and J had the courage to look what they were doing squarely in the face and call it by its proper name.

It was also a relief to know that Elva's fate had been decided. He was not quite indifferent to the idea of her death, not after what there had been between them. He was much less indifferent to all the deaths her treason had caused. Elva Thompson would be no real loss to anyone except her masters in Russland.

R went on. "There's another project I want started, and I want you on it."

"What's that, sir?"

"Contingency planning for action against the dragons, when they start landing in Englor."

"*When,* sir?"

"I believe Miss Haran, Blade. Don't you?"

Blade laughed. "Absolutely, sir. But—isn't this intruding on the Plans and Operations people?"

"It is. But with General Strong's attitude, I doubt if one single lieutenant is going to be assigned to plan how to fight off dragons. That's going to mean trouble when they land, no matter how much planning we can do at Special Operations. But if we do something, it may cut the damage." He smiled grimly. "Also, it will help tighten the noose around the neck of our mutual friend General Sir Morgan Strong."

Chapter 19

Lieutenant Colonel Michael Morris, commanding officer of the Second Battalion, Duke of Pembroke's Own Light Infantry, was bored. This was not an uncommon or unexpected situation, even in wartime and even for a field-grade officer. He still didn't care for it.

It was waiting for orders that had become boring. The battalion was assigned to the Seventy-first Infantry Brigade, one of five brigades trained and equipped to operate out of helicopters. Three of the others already formed the First Airmobile Division, assigned to the Eighth Army in Gallia. The rumor was that one more of the airmobile brigades would be assigned to Eighth Army reserve. Would it be the Seventy-first Brigade or the Fifty-ninth, down in Cornwall?

Morris hoped it would be the Seventy-first. After thirty years in the army, it was maddening to come to the edge of war in command of a fine battalion without being sure of being able to take it into action.

He rose from his chair, buttoned up his field jacket, picked up his swagger stick, and headed for the door of the hut. A little walk would put some fresh air into his lungs and perhaps push some of the boredom out of his mind. Then a drink in the messhall, or perhaps two—no more than that—and then to bed. He pushed open the door and stepped out into the night.

As he did, he sensed something large and dark passing low overhead, something also long and thin. He caught a glimpse of what seemed to be broad wings spreading far out on either side. That made no sense. Neither airplanes nor helicopters made so little noise when they were so low, and who would be coming down in a glider here at this time of night? Who, except—? Then Colonel Morris snatched his sidearm from its holster and broke into a run. The damned Russlanders were staging a glider raid!

He'd taken barely half a dozen steps when a raw orange light flared in the darkness ahead among the tents of the battalion's rifle companies. Screams of pain and terror rose along with the light. Colonel Morris stopped dead, his eyes telling him what was moving among the tents but his mind refusing to register the message.

A dragon towered there among the tents, a dragon that might have escaped from some illustration in a book of tales for children. A fanged and scaled head rose on a long neck, with great yellow eyes glaring out on either side of the long snout. From that snout, orange flame roared like the jet from a flamethrower. Morris smelled the raw, wrenching foulness of methane and gagged as the dragon belched flame again.

The neck swept down into a massive body supported on four claw-footed legs, now spread wide. Morris found his stomach quivering as he caught sight of a soldier writhing under one of those feet, blood oozing from him as the dragon's weight slowly crushed him into the ground.

Behind the body a long tail stretched off into the

darkness, and on either side of the body spread immense wings. Morris saw one of those wings lash forward into the faces of half a dozen soldiers as they scrambled out of their tent. They stopped. The great head swung toward them, the flames gushed out, and more screams rose horribly into the night. Four of the men went down, writhing and rolling frantically. Two panicked and ran, flames streaming from hair and clothing.

They did not get far. Out of the darkness another dragon came sweeping down to land almost in front of them. It seemed disoriented for a moment. Hope leaped up in Colonel Morris that it would overlook the fleeing men, or miss them if it struck.

Then the great scaled head dipped, fanged jaws closed, and one of the men shrieked as the dragon lifted him high. A moment later he heard an echo as the dragon's tail smashed into the other soldier. He flew twenty feet into the air, landing with the ghastly limpness of a man whose bones have all been smashed in a single blow.

A third dragon whispered overhead, and a fourth. Somewhere a machine gun sent up tracer at the last dragon. One wing folded up in midair, and the monster plunged down to the ground faster than the others. But it moved and roared and flamed just as fiercely, no more harmed by the fall than if it had been a block of solid steel.

"Sharpshooters!" roared Morris, in a voice that would have carried over the uproar made by a dozen dragons. "Sharpshooters! Turn out and open fire! Aim for the eyes!"

Yet another orange flare in the darkness, and then a far larger one as some part of the ammunition store exploded. Bits of flaming debris arched high into the sky and dropped all around Colonel Morris, trailing smoke. The glare from the explosion lit up a fifth dragon gliding in, and then a sixth.

A new kind of light flared in the darkness, and the flame trail of an antitank rocket streaked upward. It caught the sixth dragon where the long neck joined the body. The dragon doubled up in midair and fell. It did not move when it landed, its roars were feeble, and only a tiny jet of flame flickered around its jaws.

Morris let out a shout of triumph. "They *can be killed,* men! They can be!" He had not realized until this moment that he himself had thought the dragons invulnerable, monsters from another world where nature was not as it was in this one. "Antitank and heavy weapons men, back up the sharpshooters! Everyone else stand clear and cordon off the area!"

Colonel Morris said no more, because he had no more breath. He realized that he'd been shouting more like a sergeant major on a drill field than an officer commanding a battalion. But there'd been no other way to get his orders through or relieve his own feelings of being caught up in a nightmare.

He turned and dashed back to his hut, charging through the door so fast that he nearly took it off its hinges. He snatched the telephone off the desk and furiously punched in the numbers of Brigade Headquarters.

"Hello, Brigade? Morris of the Pembrokes. We've got a spot of trouble here. The camp is under attack by fire-breathing dragons. What? I am perfectly sober, and I assure you that I am not joking.

"Yes, I said dragons. Good God, man, they've already killed at least a dozen men out of the battalion and exploded an ammunition store! We've disabled one, but there are at least five left.

"This is the third time I've said it—*dragons.* D-R-A-G-O-N-S, as in 'snapdragons.' Eh? Well, if you think there is a more appropriate term for these—monsters—I respectfully invite you to visit our camp and examine them for yourselves. If you can come up with a more appropriate term, I will gladly use it. In the meantime, I want the brigade antitank company, a helicopter patrol with flares, and at least two sections of antiaircraft rockets, at once! No, I will not stay on the telephone for the Brigadier! Good evening to you."

Colonel Morris hung up the telephone, holstered his sidearm, and drew his rifle out from under his desk. Then he threw a final look around the hut and went back outside to lead his battalion against the strangest enemy it had ever faced.

Blade gently closed his fingers on a handful of Rilla Haran's long hair and drew it across his throat. It smelled fresh and clean and felt deliciously silky against his skin. His other hand was resting lightly on the upper curve of her left breast. He moved the hand over the warm roundness, felt the nipple harden, felt a quivering in Rilla's body—

—and sat upright in the bed as a scream of raw terror sounded from outside. After that came the thud of something heavy striking the ground, a tinkling crash from the inn's greenhouse, and a second scream. There was more terror in this one, but also agonizing pain.

Now flickering orange light lit up the room, and Blade heard a peculiar faint roaring and hissing. A wave of warm, stinking air swept into the room, making the curtains dance and knocking some loose sheets of letter paper off the desk by the window.

Blade sprang out of bed, diving to the floor and rolling until he could reach under the desk. His hands closed on his rifle, an Enfield Type 7, customized and refined for sniper work. It could put its magazine of twenty rounds into a target far more precisely than any standard-issue weapon. On Rilla's advice, Blade had chosen it as the most potent antidragon weapon he could bring along on their little vacation, without looking like a walking arsenal.

Blade peered out the window. He was not surprised to see a dragon—a rather small one, from what Rilla had said—sitting in the ruins of the greenhouse. Around its neck hung one of the aluminum frames, and around its feet was a litter of smashed pots, trampled plants, splintered trays, and gardening tools. The inn's gardener lay on his back in the wreckage, torn open from throat to groin.

The dragon threw back its head and flame jetted out again. The flame struck the inn to Blade's left, out of his sight. Screams sounded over the hissing roar of the flames.

Rilla crawled around from the far side of the bed and

peered over Blade's shoulder at the dragon. "There is no quick way to get it without a grenade." She shook her head. "I knew this would come upon us soon. Why would they not believe me—?" She pressed her hands into her eyes to hide her tears and to blot out the sight of the dragon.

Blade patted her shoulder. "I've got to get out of here before I start shooting. Otherwise it'll attack the inn." He slung his rifle, heaved the window open, and scrambled out onto the sill. Then he sprang downward, before the dragon could notice him.

It was a twelve-foot drop, but he landed as lightly as a cat, sprang to his feet, and ran. He sprinted around the rear of the greenhouse, ignoring shards of glass jabbing at his bare feet, and reached the shelter of a tree. Quickly he unslung the rifle, chambered a round, took rough aim, and fired. He didn't expect to hurt the dragon with this shot, only to draw its attention away from the inn, onto himself.

The bullet smacked into the dragon somewhere along the scale-armored neck. It did no vital damage—the windpipe and spinal cord were both deep inside and sheathed in heavy cartilage. It did make the dragon swing around in the middle of breathing more fire at the inn. The last jet of flame played over the ruins of the greenhouse, setting fire to the dead gardener's clothing.

As it turned, the dragon gave Blade a perfect shot at its left eye. One could not kill a dragon with a bullet in the eye. The brain was too deep inside the skull. But one could hurt it.

This time Blade aimed as carefully as if he were shooting in competition on a range. He saw the great yellow eye suddenly disintegrate into pulp. The dragon roared without letting out any flame and twisted around, trying to get a sight of its tormentor with its remaining eye.

It did, but it also gave Blade the chance to fire another good shot. The dragon's remaining eye vanished as it surged forward. Blade sprang away from the tree as the blind dragon crashed head-first into it. The tree snapped as if it had been a sapling and crashed down, just missing Blade but not missing the inn's garage.

Now, in theory, Blade could get directly in front of the dragon and fire a shot into its mouth that would penetrate the brain. Blade hoped Rilla's theory would hold up in practice.

The dragon seemed partly stunned by the collision with the tree. It lurched back to its feet, turned its maimed head in the general direction of the smashed garage, and let out its flaming breath again. A gasoline tank erupted in one of the cars, sending flame spurting up through the holes in the roof. The dragon lurched toward the garage, drawn by the heat and the sound of the flames crackling among the dry timber.

Blade saw his chance. He chambered another round and ran as if he wanted to set a record for the hundred-yard dash. He rounded the garage, skidded to a stop, raised his rifle, and aimed at the monstrous head looming over the flaming garage. The mouth opened to spurt out more flame, Blade's finger squeezed the trigger, the rifle butt jarred his shoulder. The dragon's head jerked back as if someone had tightened a noose around its neck. The creature reared, as if trying to pluck something down from the swirling smoke overhead. Then it toppled over backward and fell with a thud that jarred Blade from top to bottom and knocked out what was left of the windows in the greenhouse.

Blade sank to his knees, bracing himself with the rifle, for a moment not sure that he could stand. He could with ease have dealt with a human opponent at the inn, or a monster like the dragon in a wilderness of mountain or jungle. To have it come out of nightmare into the sane and normal world that was Englor left him confused. And he had known about the dragons, and expected them! What would it be like for people to whom the dragons would be a total, deadly surprise? What would they do? How many of them would die or go mad tonight?

By the time he'd run these questions through his mind, Blade found that he could stand again. He rose to his feet and walked toward the dragon. He chambered another round in his rifle and held it ready. He didn't see how the dragon could still be alive, but Rilla had told him how they'd been designed to be enormously tough, almost indestructible.

As if his thoughts had brought her out, Rilla came trotting toward him, holding her overcoat around her with one hand and carrying his pants in the other. Blade looked at the pants, then looked down at himself and laughed. In his haste he'd leaped out the window and fought the dragon without putting on a stitch of clothing!

Blade put down the rifle, took the pants, and managed to pull them on just before people started swarming out of the inn to crowd around him in hysterical joy and relief.

Chapter 20

Thanks to Blade's quick action, nobody at the inn except the unfortunate gardener was dead. A dozen or so people had minor burns or doses of smoke. One man had broken a leg falling down the stairs. The landlord was a sensible man who promptly brought out a barrel of beer and a case of good whiskey. Both vanished in record time, and after that even the injured felt a good deal better.

The only people who weren't feeling better were Blade and Rilla. They were alive, the dragon was dead, the inn was safe for the moment. But how many other dragons had come down on Englor this night? How many people had died from the fury of the dragons of the Red Flames? How much destruction had they left behind them?

The telephone lines were down, Blade's car was a burned-out wreck in the garage, and there were no buses or trains for miles around. Blade and Rilla had chosen an isolated country inn for their vacation—too isolated, it seemed now.

Eventually Blade borrowed the landlord's bicycle and set off in search of some way to get back in touch with the world. He was barely out of the inn yard when an Imperial Air Force helicopter came swooping in low overhead. It hovered as it passed over the inn and caught sight of the dead dragon, then landed. Blade dashed back, just in time to greet the pilot as he climbed down from the helicopter, camera in hand.

Blade identified himself and gave the pilot an account of the night's events. The pilot congratulated Blade on killing the dragon, noted down Rilla's comments, but could tell them little about the night's events.

It was certain that an enormous number of dragons had swooped down on Englor. The pilot was on a mission to search the countryside for them, alive or dead. He'd already found several live ones in the area. People were advised to stay put until further notice. No, he couldn't take Blade and Rilla back to his base. His helicopter couldn't handle the load. But he would radio his base and see if they would help.

As the helicopter vanished into the sunrise, three Imperial Air Force jet fighters flew overhead a thousand feet up. Blade noticed they all carried pods of air-to-ground rockets slung under their wings.

The landlord grinned. "That'll fix those damned monsters if they get a sight of them. You can bet on that."

Blade nodded, wishing he could share the landlord's optimism. In the open countryside, a rocket salvo from the air could indeed blow a dragon to bits. But most of the dragons should have landed in heavily populated areas. They would be far deadlier there, also less vulnerable to heavy weapons.

Just before noon a larger helicopter landed near the inn. This one had not only room but orders to take Blade and Rilla aboard. As it carried them across the countryside toward its base, Blade was finally able to get from its crew a rough account of what had happened last night.

An enormous force of dragons had swarmed down on Englor—many hundreds, perhaps a thousand. Many of them were already dead and only a few would survive more than another day or two. The armed forces of Englor were hard at work.

Meanwhile, however, thousands of people were dead, and tens of thousands made homeless or driven into panic-stricken flight. Hundreds of buildings and even whole villages lay in ruin. Power and telephone lines, railroads, bridges were cut or blocked all up and down the whole eastern half of Englor. It was impossible to say more, for reports from areas heavily attacked by the dragons were few and seldom accurate.

Blade saw there was no point in pressing matters. The helicopter crew were able to do their duty, but they were obviously badly shaken by the night's events. The coming of the dragons seemed to have spread panic across the land. In the long run, that panic could be more deadly to Englor and to her war effort than the mere physical damage.

Blade's mind was filled with these thoughts and even grimmer ones all the way to the base.

At Special Operations Headquarters things were comparatively quiet. The area hadn't yet been attacked by any dragons. A number of the Independent Operations people and other combat-trained personnel were out reinforcing the local garrisons. No orders of any kind had come through.

That didn't bother R. He was not a man to wait for orders before starting to prepare for what might have to be done later. He started by giving Blade and Rilla a thorough briefing on the attack. He painted the same grim picture Blade had from the helicopter crew—death, destruction, panic. There was one photograph that summed up for Blade the whole nightmarish quality of the dragons' attack.

It showed Big Ben—the same in Englor as in England, spire for spire and window for window. It also showed a dragon perched high on the great tower, its claws firmly sunk into the roof, tail hanging down, head peering out over the street below and jetting flame. It was ghastly and grotesque. Blade could only feel that it was totally abominable that any of this should have happened at all, and that none of it should happen again.

"Unfortunately I think it will happen again, and soon," said Rilla. "They have used no more than a thousand dragons in this attack. There should be at least three times that many in the bases in the Nordsbergen mountains. There will also be twice as many again in the breeding pens in Russland. The production rate will be over a thousand a month."

Blade grimaced. He knew all this already, but it took on new and horrible dimensions in the wake of the night's attack. "So—we are planning on the basis of further attacks?"

R nodded. "I am going to set up a series of briefings on dragon-fighting tactics, starring you and Rilla. We haven't been asked for them yet, but I'm quite sure we will be after the next attack. I am also going to organize a mobile defense for this Headquarters. Your promotion to lieutenant colonel has come through, so I'd like to put you in charge of it."

"Very good, sir."

A second attack came two days later, only a few hundred dragons but concentrated almost entirely on London. What the first attack hadn't done to touch off a national panic, the second did. At least two-hundred thousand people left London the next day, or tried to. Roads and railroad stations were packed, and the traffic jams brought all military movements to a complete halt. Thousands of troops had to be called in to get traffic moving again, keep order, and prevent looting and fires. A whole infantry division that was about to sail for Gallia had its orders canceled.

R never looked really worried, but he looked rather ill-at-ease after reading the reports of the second dragon attack. "I begin to suspect what the Red Flames are planning. They want to force us to tie down troops for the defense of Englor instead of sending them to the Eighth Army in Gallia. Those defense troops in turn will have to be dispersed all over the country, to guard against the dragons.

"That makes no sense, of course. But all the average man can see is that he has to have a squad of soldiers camped on the vicar's lawn, in case the dragons come again. If he can't get that he'll panic. That will make a thorough shambles of the war effort."

Blade and Rilla held their first briefing two days later. Rilla spoke from behind a screen, through a microphone fitted with a scrambler to disguise her voice. R was taking no avoidable chances on the Red Flames' being able to trace their prize defector.

Blade led off the briefing. He strode up to the speaker's stand, turned on the microphone, and stared down at the audience. A hundred high-ranking officers and civilians stared back at him. He cleared his throat and began.

"The Empire of Englor is under attack by artificially mutated dragons, produced by mass cloning methods at a facility in Russland. They are then transported to bases high in the mountains of Nordsbergen and launched across the Nord Sea. Their glide ratio is sufficient to bring them across the sea to the shores of Englor. After that, they seek targets of opportunity, using against such targets teeth, claws, tails, and the exhalation of burning methane from their gastrointestinal tracts.

"They are animals in appearance, but in another sense they are not animals. They are military machines, constructed of biological materials by biological methods, in much the same way as a tank is built in a factory out of steel and rubber. We face—"

And so on. Each briefing lasted two hours, and there were three of them that day. By the end of the third, Blade felt as weary and dry as if he'd fought in a pitched battle. He and Rilla each drained a pitcher of beer and emptied a plate of sausages before they felt like speaking again.

After the meal, R drew Blade aside.

"I think you've done as much as you can expect to do in the briefings. What I want you to do now is take command of a group of about fifty of our combat people. We're going to send you down to Norfolk.

"We are going to try using our shadow headquarters as bait in an experiment, to see if the dragons can be drawn to specific points where we're ready to meet them. Your old friend Elva Thompson is going to have a role in this experiment, although she won't realize it.

"We are going to 'activate' the Norfolk facility, sending down a contingent of staff people and an assortment of files that will look important. I will add to this window-dressing by going down there myself.

"Your men will be stationed at various points in the general area, to move in against the dragons by helicopter or by fast boat. I'll have a small squad of combat men to hold down things at the headquarters itself. I think we can see to it that Elva Thompson won't know this. I also think we can see to it that she doesn't survive the night's fighting."

That was the essence of the plan, and the details followed in swift and precise succession. As Blade left to join Rilla, it struck him what a bold, original, and flexible plan R had developed.

In fact, it was just the sort of plan that Blade would have expected from J.

Chapter 21

Elva Thompson showed her identification to the sentry at the gate. He scanned it by the faint light of a hooded flashlight. Elva had to fight to keep a smile off her lips. The blackout would not save the Special Operations compound when the dragons came. It would make it easier for her to slip out into the countryside and call the dragons down out of the sky.

"Sure you want to go out tonight, Miss Thompson? The weather's making up for a storm."

"Thank you, corporal. But I've spent just a few too many hours at my desk. I need to take a walk and unwind."

"All right, miss. I'll log you out. Don't go too far down the path to the left. The river's up a bit and the ground's gone bad."

"Thank you. I'll be careful." The corporal opened the gate for her and she strode out of the compound. The gravel of the parking lot crunched under her feet.

Elva crossed the parking lot at a leisurely walk. By the time she'd reached the far side of the lot, she was out of sight from the gate. She swung to the right and broke into a steady lope that was almost a run.

Her goal was a field two miles to the north, a field bordered on the east by a long thin strip of woods. In those woods she'd concealed the equipment for tonight's work.

Each dragon landing tonight had a small radio receiver surgically implanted in its skull. In the woods Elva had a portable transmitter, broadcasting on a selection of wavelengths that the dragons' receivers could pick up. On some of those wavelengths she could activate the pleasure centers of the dragons' brains, to draw them irresistably toward her. On other wavelengths she would work on the pain centers, driving the dragons into a fury.

Tonight she would use pleasure to bring the dragons out of the sky, practically on top of the compound, then use pain to drive them mad. They would rampage about the area, smashing and slaying everything in their paths. Then she would turn on the pleasure again. The dragons would become as harmless as lambs while she moved about freely, gathering up files and films from the ruins of the headquarters.

Then there would be pain again, and the dragons on the loose to spread terror and destruction across the countryside. As the dragons cleared a path for her, she would at last make her way to the river to wait for her rescuers.

She hoped she would not have to wait long. She had done well for the Red Flames. So she felt she deserved all the rewards they'd promised her. She wouldn't say that out loud, of course. General Golovin had a reputation for dealing harshly with those he thought were getting greedy. But General Golovin was not the only man with power in Russland. If necessary, she could earn the gratitude and support of some of the others.

After a while she had to leave the path and cut across country. The long grass was already wet with the night's dew and quickly dampened her slacks up to the knee, while brambles jabbed their thorns into her.

The mile of cross-country walking slowed her, but she still had plenty of time when she reached the field. It stretched before her, dark and empty and agreeably silent.

On the far side the trees rose in a forbidding wall. She lay down, watching for any sign of ambush.

The darkness and the silence remained unbroken. Crouching low, she made her way across the field. With a sigh of relief she grasped the handles of the transmitter and dragged it out of its hiding place. It weighed less than thirty pounds, so it had been easy for her to carry it to the woods. Now it was easy for her to carry it back out again.

On top of the transmitter was a small balloon. Elva pulled the cord to inflate it, and watched while it swelled into a six-foot sphere of dark plastic. Then she carried it out into the open and released it. It rose into the night, the antenna wire trailing behind it. She waited until the antenna was fully unreeled, activated the transmitter, and set the frequency selector to one of the pleasure wavelengths.

Then she leaned back against the moss-grown trunk of an elm. Her work was done for the moment. She looked at her watch. The signals pouring out into the night should be reaching the dragons now. The leading wave of tonight's attack should be no more than twenty miles offshore.

Richard Blade stood on the bridge of the motor torpedo boat, staring up into the sky and listening to the reports as they came in over the radio. He knew there was no good reason for staring at the sky yet. The nearest dragons would still be well out of sight. Watching the sky merely eased the strain of waiting.

With every minute, a new report of dragons came in from the radar stations along the coast or from the patrol planes offshore. The young lieutenant in command of the torpedo boat was beginning to fidget.

"Damn it," he finally muttered. "Why can't the planes hit the dragons before they land? It makes more sense to get them in the air."

Blade hesitated, not wanting to reveal information that was not yet in general circulation. But he happened to know that the lieutenant came from an East Coast town. His wife and baby daughter were there now, where the dragons might land tonight. The man had a right to know at least some of the truth.

"They aren't a good target for missiles," said Blade. "If a plane slows down enough to hit them with its guns, it's likely to stall out and crash. Antiaircraft guns can pick them off while they're in the air, but there aren't enough antiaircraft guns." The lieutenant nodded, obviously wishing that things were otherwise, but was silent.

Blade's eyes swept forward and aft along the boat's deck. The sailors were at the bow and stern cannon, in their helmets and flak vests. His own men sat on the torpedo tubes or leaned against the superstructure. Each man carried an Uzi and a light antitank rocket launcher. The decks were piled with extra rocket rounds and ammunition cans. Blade hoped no dragon would get a good breath of flame onto that deck. The fireworks would be spectacular and deadly.

He checked his own weapons. Blade carried his Enfield 7 rifle, now fitted with infrared telescopic sights, a heavy revolver, hand grenades, and a flare pistol.

More minutes, more reports. Then suddenly the lieutenant pointed a shaking hand upward into the darkness. Blade raised his eyes from the man's pale face and also stared upward.

Dim but unmistakable in the night, three dragons were gliding in across the river. They came and went so fast that they might have seemed ghosts if the radar operator hadn't called in.

"Sir, it looks like they're heading upriver. Estimate landing point about ten miles west."

"Very good. Keep tracking them until they go off the screen."

Before the first three dragons went off the screen more swept in from the sea, three, six, ten at a time. All were following nearly the same path as the first three.

The lieutenant smiled shakily. "The buggers are going to be landing right on top of each other if they aren't careful." It was a weak joke delivered in a weak voice. Blade said nothing.

Still more minutes, more reports, and more dragons. Blade found himself coming alert at the slightest noise.

His reason told him that the dragons could not attack the boat from a thousand feet up. His instincts told him that it would be death to attract the notice of a single one of those monsters gliding eerily overhead.

Blade stopped thinking of minutes. Time became something long and formless, without beginning or end.

Then the speaker crackled. "Radio message, sir. Dagger to Buckle Teams. Hollyhock."

Blade grinned. "Dagger" was R, and the "Buckle Teams" were his own striking force in their helicopters and boats. "Hollyhock" was the order to move in. R had reached his decision about where the dragons were landing. Now the trap was going to close.

Blade slapped the lieutenant on the shoulder. "Let's get underway. Up the river, standard cruising speed."

"Aye, aye, colonel."

The engines rumbled into life and the deck began to vibrate, then tilted gently aft as the boat got underway. Blade clung to the bridge railing and the grin on his face grew broader.

It felt good to be springing the trap, instead of having one sprung on him.

Elva Thompson straddled the branch, counting dragons. She stopped when she'd counted a hundred, landing in the field or passing so low overhead that they were certainly about to land. Then she scrambled down the tree, so fast that she tore her slacks all along the inside of one thigh.

She ran quickly to the transmitter. The dials showed that everything was still working, and the batteries had a good hour's life still in them. That would be more than enough time to finish her work.

She lifted the transmitter and hooked the carrying straps over her shoulders and around her waist. Her hand reached for the main knob that would turn the broadcast wavelength from pleasure to pain, turn the dragons from docile to furious. The hand wavered for a moment, then twisted the knob.

Pain roared and thundered in the brains and along the nerves of all the dragons. They roared and thundered in turn. Elva clapped her hands over her ears as the sound filled the darkness all around her. It seemed that the ground itself was shaking so that the trees might fall down on top of her and crush her into the earth.

Then the roaring and thundering of the dragons started finding echoes. Elva listened, in surprise and confusion and mounting fear. There shouldn't be any such thing as the sounds swelling in the air high above.

Then fear swamped her as she recognized the sounds. Rockets were coming down out of the sky at the dragons—at her. They might have been launched from the air, from the ground, even from the sea that was so close and had promised a road to safety. She didn't know or care. She only knew that the rockets had been launched, and now they were about to land.

She would have broken into a run, dashing in panic for the river or anyplace else away from the sound of the rockets. But her legs would not move. She pressed herself against a tree for support—transmitter, dragons, mission and everything else but the rockets totally forgotten.

Then the night was full of flame and thunder, as the rockets landed.

The bridge of the torpedo boat wasn't high enough to give Blade the view he wanted. He climbed up the mast and braced himself on the mounting for the radar. It was a precarious perch. The torpedo boat was working up to more than thirty knots, vibrating wildly and lurching sickeningly from side to side every time it rounded a bend in the river. Blade had to cling with both hands to the mast to keep from being shaken to the deck or even straight over the side.

He was holding on when the rockets arched across the sky and exploded among the dragons. He saw the yellow flames of the explosions and the blazing silver trails of white phosphorus. He saw dragons thrown into the air, some whole, some in pieces. He saw others knocked out of the air by the concussion, to land among the writhing remains of their comrades. He saw the orange fire-breath of the dragons, now pitiful instead of terrifying. He saw all this, and he wondered if there was going to be anything for his own men to do. It looked as if the salvos of artillery rockets R had called in on the dragons' main landing site might do nearly all that would be needed.

There was no way to be sure about that, not without men going over the ground with weapons in their hands to deal with whatever might be left. Blade scrambled down the mast and into the radio room to get reports from the other Buckle Teams.

One by one they checked in. One by one they reported dead dragons all over the place, but plenty of live ones as well. They were going into action, and Blade wished them good luck and good hunting. He didn't need to do anything else. Picked men from Special Operations and the Imperial Marine Commandos could fight anything, without officers looking over their shoulders.

The rocket trails flamed across the sky for a few more minutes, then stopped. R didn't want to risk hitting the Buckle Teams as they moved in against the dragons. Then the radio crackled again, and it was R's own voice that Blade heard coming over the air.

"Dagger to Buckle One. We have reports of an unidentified small craft seen heading upriver about half an hour ago. Also, Imperial Navy Patrol Craft 991 reports a probable submarine contact off the estuary. Suggests possible attempt to land or extract saboteurs under cover of dragon operations."

"Buckle One to Dagger. Description of small craft."

"Dagger to Buckle One. Estimate is standard Russland folding assault boat with outboard motor. Crew and armament unknown. Continue to give first priority to operations against dragons in your area."

As Blade hung up the earphones, he heard the torpedo boat's engines suddenly slow. A moment later he had to grab the battle light to brace himself as the boat swung into a sharp turn. He was still holding on for balance when both bow and stern guns cut loose with an ear-splitting *pom-pom-pom*. Smoke swirled in through the hatch as Blade hauled himself furiously up the ladder.

As his head thrust into the open, he saw the whole deck lit up by the streams of tracer spewed out by the boat's deck guns. The light shells were tearing into a dragon lurching along the bank. It dragged itself a few more yards, then collapsed and rolled into the water with a sullen splash.

Another dragon reared up from behind a line of trees, flame licking out from its mouth. The jet of flame leaped across the water toward the boat, but couldn't reach all the way. Two of the rocket launchers went off together and both rockets took the dragon in the mouth. The dragon's long neck still heaved up and down, but suddenly there was no longer a head on it. The guns swung toward the maimed dragon, chopping into its body.

Blade sprang down onto the deck and unslung his rifle. The battle against the dragons was joined now. The range was long for sharpshooting under these conditions, but Blade did not want to be left out of the battle. He was too much of a hunter by instinct. Another dragon loomed up on the opposite side of the river, the rifle came up, Blade's eye clamped to the sight, and his finger tightened on the trigger.

Elva Thompson was walking toward the river. After two miles she no longer had the breath to run. She could only be sure her legs were still attached to her body because pain stabbed through them every time she took a step.

She stumbled on, tearing through a prickly hedge. By the time she was clear of it, one sleeve of her blouse and one leg of her slacks were ripped from her body. She thought: "At this rate I'll show up on the river bank with no more clothes on than a Palladium stripteaser." The thought did not stop or slow her. It could not, as long as the thought of reaching the river drew her onward. She'd survived the rockets, she'd survived the slaughter of the dragons, she'd been able to get rid of the transmitter. After all that, she wasn't going to let a simple cross-country run defeat her.

She half-scrambled, half-rolled down a bank into a ditch filled with stagnant water. She arose shivering and soaked to the skin, the slime stinging her cuts and scrapes. She staggered across the road, aware that she was in full view but ignoring it. She knew the road. On the other side of it lay the last stretch of woodland and field before the river.

Elva was unaware of crossing that last stretch. It seemed to her that she crossed it in a single leap, to find herself by the river bank. She held on to a branch and craned her neck. She almost lost her grip when she saw the slim black assault boat with the two men in it, snugged close against the bank just upstream. She managed to hold on with one hand and use the other to signal. The boat slid across the water toward her, and one of the men rose from his seat to help her down into it. She huddled between his knees, bent almost double, as the other man opened the throttle wide. The boat lifted as suddenly and as violently as if it was going to take off like a seaplane, the bow rising and the stern digging in. They raced out into the river and headed downstream.

Elva felt an immense release of the tension and the pain that had filled her for so long. Not a complete release, though—not yet. They still had to reach the sea and the submarine waiting for them. Was the river defended as the land had been? Someone had learned enough to lay a murderous ambush for the dragons. Had they learned everything? For a moment fear stabbed at her again.

The fear was fading again as the assault boat swept around a bend in the river. Elva looked ahead—and all her breath tore itself out of her body in one terrible shriek.

The assault boat and the motor torpedo boat were each doing nearly thirty knots. So it was at a combined speed of nearly sixty knots that they met bows-on, and the torpedo boat pounded the smaller craft out of existence. Elva Thompson had no time for any last thoughts or words. Death came at her too swiftly, as the torpedo boat smashed her down into the depths of the river before she could do more than scream.

The woman's scream from the water died as the torpedo boat roared on. It still seemed to linger in the air and in the ears and minds of every man aboard the torpedo boat. Blade was the first man to shake himself free of its spell. Even he wasn't quite in time to see the dead dragon floating in the river ahead.

The dragon was dead, but it was still a ten-ton mass of armored flesh. Ramming it at thirty knots was like ramming a solid log. The torpedo boat bounced wildly, with a deafening booming and clanging of strained and twisted metal. The shock knocked everyone aboard flat, Blade included. Ammunition boxes, weapons, helmets, and men skittered wildly along the deck. By some miracle no one fell overboard.

Then the boat rode up over the dragon and plunged into the water on the far side. It dug its bow in until the spray soaked the men at the forward gun. With a hideous metallic screech one propeller tore free of its shaft, caught in the dragon's scaly hide. The propeller shaft was already spinning at nearly top speed. Now, with the shaft suddenly freed of the propeller's weight, the engine ran wild. Its rumble turned into a whine and the whine into a shrill scream. Before the men at the controls could cut the throttle, the scream ended in a deafening bang as the runaway engine exploded.

The men in the engine room died instantly, from the concussion or from the jagged bits of metal that flew in all directions. The metal flew on. It flew up through the decks, hitting several men there but by some miracle not hitting any of the ammunition. It flew out through the hull, tearing a dozen jagged holes. It flew downward, rupturing fuel tanks and lines, which promptly poured their contents over arcing electrical circuits. Flames roared up, fighting against the inrushing water.

The boat began to slow as the water flooded in. Blade rose to his feet, aware of aches and pains in various parts of his body but indifferent to all of them, and started shouting orders.

"Get that ammunition overboard! Fast! If the fire catches it—"

He didn't need to finish. All those men who could still move and grab something started picking up rocket rounds and ammunition cans and heaving them into the river. Along with the splashes Blade could hear the growing roar of the flames below. He'd hoped the water might put them out, but apparently the burning fuel was rising on top of the water.

The torpedo boat was beyond saving. Time to get off. Blade pulled himself painfully up onto the bridge, cupped his hands, and began shouting:

"All hands, abandon ship! Abandon ship! Make for the south shore! Hold on to your Uzis if you can."

"Aye, aye," came back from all along the deck. Blade saw men stripping off helmets and flak vests, tightening the straps on life jackets, bending to help wounded comrades. The young lieutenant was slumped over the control panel, with an ugly purple lump on his left temple. Blade grabbed him around the shoulders and pulled the man erect.

As he did, a blast of hot air roared up around them from below, and flames followed a moment later. They would have cremated the lieutenant where he stood, if Blade hadn't dragged him clear in time.

Carrying the lieutenant, Blade scrambled down the ladder on the outside of the bridge. The deck was deserted, except for the dead, and beginning to buckle and twist under the growing heat from below. It was time to go. Blade pulled on his own life jacket and strapped another around the unconscious man. Then he lowered him over the side and slid into the water himself. The torpedo boat was so flooded that by now the deck was only two feet above the water.

The chill water of the river revived the lieutenant. His eyes flickered open, taking in Blade first, then the rest of the scene around him, including his sinking boat. His eyes closed again, as if he wanted to shut out the sight. Blade knew that a captain who is losing his ship seldom feels much like talking and said nothing. He struck out for the south bank, towing the lieutenant with one hand and holding his rifle out of the water with the other.

A hundred yards of chill water lay between Blade and the south bank, and the current was strong. They'd covered about half the distance when Blade saw something dark bobbing on the surface just ahead. Another few kicks, and he recognized a body. A few more, and he recognized Elva Thompson.

So it had been her death scream splitting the darkness. Blade was glad that she was dead, but also glad of the darkness. A woman battered and drowned and perhaps slashed by the torpedo boat's propellers would not be something he wanted to see too clearly. Not when he'd held that woman in his arms with desire and even with affection.

He swam on toward the bank. Eventually it loomed up ahead of him. Hands reached down to help the lieutenant, and Blade scrambled up after him.

Blade formed the survivors into a rough defensive perimeter and settled down to wait. There was nothing they could do with his rifle and the Uzis except defend themselves, and even that might be a problem if the dragons came at them in force.

They saw no dragons nearer than the far bank of the river. Gradually the roars and bellows and screams of raging and dying dragons faded away. They began to hear the sound of boats coming up the river and helicopters flitting low over the trees, searching the area. It was one of those helicopters that found them half an hour later, and one of the boats that took them away to medical care, dry clothing, and hot tea.

Chapter 22

Blade had cuts and bruises and a sore wrist. The doctors bandaged the wrist and let him go. He was in excellent shape to take part in the staff conferences that began meeting the next day to answer the burning question:

What Do We Do About the Dragons of the Red Flames?

The night's work had been a roaring success—two hundred dragons dead, and only light losses in Englor. But they'd been able to lay a near-perfect trap for the dragons, and that might not happen again. So last night's success really proved nothing.

It was possible to stand on the defensive. The east coast of Englor could be lined with radar stations, antiaircraft weapons, and soldiers, until few dragons could land safely or live long enough to do any damage.

It was also possible to attack the bases in the mountains of Nordsbergen, where the dragons were kept in great prefabricated domes (the ones Blade had thought might be for radar sets) until it was time to launch them on their flights across the Nord Sea. A steady bombardment from the air could kill a good many dragons and make the bases useless.

Those were the two most popular ideas. R, Blade, and Rilla were at first the only people supporting a third and much bolder proposal. They suggested flying a commando force straight into Russland aboard the VTOL assault transports. Such a force could destroy the breeding facilities, pens, and laboratories. It could kill or capture most of the key people in the whole Red Flame genetic-warfare program. At one blow it could end the threat of the dragons and set the Red Flames back ten years in their program to breed monsters for their war against Englor.

It would certainly be a bold stroke—too bold, in the opinion of too many high-ranking civilians and military men. Even R was pessimistic at first about getting his plan adopted. Then suddenly it acquired two high-ranking supporters.

One supporter was the field marshal commanding the Eighth Army in Gallia. He pointed out how many men and weapons would be needed to effectively defend Englor against the dragons. If that much strength was to be tied down on home-defense duties, he could not guarantee the survival of the Eighth Army in the face of a Red Flame attack. If a passive defense of Englor was to be adopted, he would respectfully request to be relieved of his command.

The other supporter for the commando raid was the air marshal who led Bomber Command of the Imperial Air Force. Attacking the Nordsbergen bases, he said, would commit bombers to repeated strikes against targets that would be more heavily defended each time. The losses would mount steadily. If he was called on to send his bombers on such missions, he would not take responsibility for keeping Bomber Command an effective force for operations against Russland. In such a situation he also would ask to be relieved of his command.

Both the field marshal and the air marshal were officers of long service and high distinction who had the ear of the Emperor himself. Soon the word went around that His Imperial Majesty was in favor of launching a direct attack on the breeding base in Russland.

After that, R and Blade had no shortage of supporters.

Their target was vulnerable for several reasons. First, it lay in the far south of Russland, where there were few enemy air bases and no real radar network. It was, however, less than an hour's flight from the sea. Within a hundred miles off the coast were a number of islands with plenty of room for the assault transports to land. Imperial submarines towing flexible fuel tanks could temporily establish a secret base on one of those islands. From the islands a fully loaded assault transport could easily reach the breeding base, land its men, and bring them out again.

Second, the base itself was weakly garrisoned. The Red Flames preferred to rely on its isolation to protect it. The garrison consisted of picked Security troops, but only about four hundred of them. They were also dispersed all over a facility that covered several square miles. A heavily armed mobile force landing from the air should have no trouble crushing the garrison.

Third, the dragon pens were uniquely vulnerable. All the thousands of dragons lived in caves on either side of a deep canyon near the laboratories. They could move about freely on the bottom of the canyon, but they could reach the surface only through a few narrow tunnels.

At the head of the canyon stood a high dam. It lowered the river until the entrances to the caves in the canyon walls were above water. It also provided electric power for the whole base.

Behind the dam lay a deep lake, several miles long and hundreds of feet deep. If the dam were blown, the waters of the lake would go roaring down the canyon, submerging the lower entrances to the dragons' caves. If at the same time the upper entrances were blown in, all the dragons penned in the caves would be trapped. Long before the river went down or the tunnels were dug free, they would suffocate, to the last dragon.

The demolition would need a large quantity of high explosives, and it would have to be precisely placed by skilled men. But both were available, both could be carried to the breeding base, and the job could be done. If it was done, the dragons of the Red Flames would not trouble Englor again.

So planning for the raid began, and the arguments began soon afterward. For example, the assault transports were highly secret. It was imperative that they be fully rigged for demolition, so that if one of them crashed or couldn't take off, it would not fall into Red Flame hands. But the assault transports were also large. Enough demolition charges to thoroughly destroy one would weigh a good deal. The weight would cut into its payload for the raid. Where was the balance point between payload and precautions, if there was one?

The planners argued over large questions, small questions, and questions that Richard Blade found it hard to believe grown men could take seriously. At times it seemed that the arguments would go on until the assault transports were all obsolete and all the dragons were dead of old age.

Eventually a plan emerged. Nine assault transports would carry deep into Russland a force of six hundred men, divided into three Groups.

The Battle Group would land at the laboratories and the breeding pens. Most of the men would be riding lightweight motorcycles, so that they could move faster and carry more ammunition. They would be supported by a number of light armored vehicles with guns and rockets. Their mission was to wipe out the garrison, capture or kill the whole staff of the base, carry off everything that could be carried off, and destroy everything else.

The Demolition Group would land at the entrance to the tunnels and around the dam. The tunnel entrances would be blown in first. Then explosives would be lowered down the inner face of the dam and detonated. The pressure of the water would do the rest.

Finally, a small Blocking Group would hold the road and railroad that led out of the base to the nearest enemy garrison. They would be able to do most of the job by blowing up two bridges across small canyons.

Two of the assault transports converted into flying tankers would accompany the nine troop carriers. They would refuel in the air a strike of twelve attack planes launched from an Imperial carrier well out to sea. The attack planes would attack the nearest enemy airbase, making it unusable. Then they would fly air cover over the dragon base while the ground troops did their work.

The attack planes would not have the range to return to their carrier after that. So their pilots would bail out at low altitude, to land among the Battle Group and be picked up by its mobile troops. They would fly out in the assault transports along with the rest of the surviving raiders.

As many as half the raiders might become casualties. All the vehicles would also be left behind, carefully booby-trapped, to lighten the transports for the flight out. But in return for three hundred men and two hundred vehicles, the ability of the Red Flames of Russland to wage genetic warfare would be destroyed for many years.

No one seemed to doubt that this was a fair trade.

No one seemed to doubt either that Lieutenant Colonel Richard Blade should be in command of the raiding force. By Imperial Special Order he was given the acting rank of full colonel. After that he settled down to the grueling routine of training his handpicked six hundred for their great day.

He hardly had a moment to spare for Rilla during that time. He did observe that she seemed both happy and sad at the same time. Happy, because the dragon base to her meant the corruption and perversion of the great discoveries she'd made in genetics. Now it was about to be destroyed. Sad, because in that destruction would die many who had been her friends and colleagues for years, and she could not be totally indifferent to their fate. Blade thought it was perhaps just as well that he and Rilla were not seeing much of each other now. It was certainly good that she was not going on the raid herself.

Blade did have time to consider one amusing fact about his position. He'd been quite certain that Englor would offer him no opportunity to rise swiftly in rank and status. Yet here he was, risen from recruit to full colonel in only a few months, given one of the choicest assignments possible for an officer of his rank.

Perhaps this was not quite so great a rise as one from slave to prince. But no man could say that Blade had not risen, and many in Englor were saying he would rise farther still if he lived long enough.

Chapter 23

Six hundred soldiers have to learn only so much in order to carry out even the most complicated operation. Even training for fifteen hours a day, six days a week, comes to an end sooner or later. Then there's nothing left to do but load the men aboard whatever is taking them to battle.

The night before Strike Force Blade took off, R took Blade out to dinner. It was a hasty dinner—too hasty, for the food and the wine both deserved a leisurely appreciation that neither man could afford to give them. Like the rest of the Strike Force, Blade had forty-eight hours' leave, and from the restaurant he would be joining Rilla. R obviously knew this, but was so much a gentleman about Blade's personal affairs that it was impossible to tell if he approved or disapproved. That was one more quality that R shared with J.

The dinner lasted long enough for R to become more talkative than usual. Perhaps it was the wine, perhaps it was the frustration at having to leave the rest of the fight against the dragons to younger men who would go where he no longer could. Whatever was working inside him, R said a great deal, almost certainly much more than he'd intended.

Blade did not remember much of it. He had an excellent memory, but he could also forget things when it seemed wise. One thing he didn't forget, and he knew afterward that he couldn't have forgotten it if he'd wanted to.

"You know something, Richard?" said R. "I had a son."

That was a surprise to Blade. He sensed that R was not expecting any reply, just continued attention.

"Yes, I had a son. He was an Independent, like you, like me. He went off to Rodzmania on an assignment, like you. Only he didn't come back. That was ten years ago. If he'd lived, he would have been about your age, I think."

R reached inside his coat with a hand that trembled slightly and drew out a small flat leather case. Blade looked down. It was his own face that stared back at him from the picture in the case—his own face, a few years younger.

"I see," he said, and nodded. Perhaps there were more profound words, but none of them came to mind now. There was still some wine in Blade's glass. He picked it up and sipped.

One thought did pop into his mind. Should he take the chance to ask what R really knew about the man called Colonel Richard Blade? Might R now let slip what he knew about Blade's origins—if he knew anything at all?

Then the thought sank back out of Blade's mind. The answer to that question was the same as always. R might reveal some of his own past, some of his own motives. He would never reveal any of his professional secrets. He would never reveal whether or not he knew that Richard Blade had come to Englor from another Dimension.

Blade sighed, picked up the wine bottle, and poured until both his glass and R's were full again.

With Strike Force Blade aboard, the assault transports flew south to a base in West Africa. They flew across the continent to another base on the east coast. They flew those two legs of their journey at high altitude, to save fuel.

They flew north from the coastal base in darkness, keeping low. At seven hundred miles an hour they raced across the dark sea toward the secret island base off the southern coast of Russland. Once a circle of ships appeared on the radar, then dropped astern. The Imperial carrier and her escorts were on station, ready to launch the attack planes on schedule.

The island came out of the night at them. The transports shifted from horizontal to vertical flight and sank down through a thousand feet of air to safe landings on the rocky top of the island. The fuel was waiting for them in great flexible bladders, towed submerged across the sea by Imperial submarines and anchored to the rocks offshore. Pumps whined in the darkness, fuel lines stiffened, gauges registered the hundreds and thousands of gallons pouring into the tanks. One by one each transport reported "Full Up." One by one they lifted into the darkness with an ear-cracking howl of jets and orange flares of exhaust. As Blade watched, the jet flares reminded him strangely of the flaming breath of the dragons.

Then his own transport rose to join the others. They burned navigation lights until the formation was complete. Then they shifted power back from vertical lift to horizontal thrust and headed toward the coast of Russland. A few minutes later the two tankers made rendezvous and swung into place at the rear of the formation. Now there were eleven of the metal giants on their way to Russland.

The coast passed below as the eastern sky began to pale. As the sky showed pink, the transports began to climb slowly. They kept a thousand feet above the ground as it rose into the rugged tableland that made up the heart of South Russland.

The land below showed few colors even as daylight spread across it. Browns and tans, grays, and an occasional flash of red or black that came and went so fast it was hard to believe it had ever been there. Small ranges of jagged peaks, like giant boulders set on end. Dry canyons and some with faint silver trickles of water in the bottom. Scarred and fissured cliffs plunging down five hundred feet. No vegetation, no sign of human life. A harsh, ugly, unnatural landscape, one that seemed to Blade an entirely appropriate setting for the dragons. They also were harsh, ugly, and unnatural.

An isolated mountain loomed on the horizon—an immense, rugged volcanic cone, its upper slopes snow covered. The troop carriers swung to the west of the mountain, the tankers to the east, heading for their fueling rendezvous with the carrier strike. Blade looked at the clock. The attack planes should be only a few minutes from their target now.

The volcanic mountain sank below the horizon again. Now the nine troop carriers split into two groups on diverging courses. The dragon base was still out of sight, ten minutes away. The transports would pass around it to the east and the west, swinging well clear of its antiaircraft defenses, then come in from the north.

The maneuver was carried out with professional smoothness, in complete radio silence. One minute Blade looked out the cockpit windows and saw eight transports in a line stretching off to the east. The next minute he saw only four. Seven minutes to go. He checked his weapons, then wished the pilots good luck and climbed down to the cargo deck.

The men were already mounted up and ready, forty on motorcycles, the rest in the vehicles of the Command Section—two armored cars, a jeep, and a radio truck. Blade passed quickly along the deck. Some of the cycle troops had already released their tie-downs. They weren't supposed to do that until the transport went on vertical flight. But if being able to save a few seconds in getting out after touchdown made them feel better—

The cargo deck was a dark, windowless metal tube. Blade had to follow the last stages of the approach to the target over the intercom. At five minutes the pilot reported the base in sight. At four minutes he reported that the two transports carrying the Demolition Group were going to vertical flight. No sign of enemy resistance yet.

Silence for two more minutes, as the three remaining transports of the western group swung around to the north of the base. Blade would have liked to hear something, but the pilot was a busy man.

Two minutes, and now Blade needed no words over the intercom to know what was happening. The note of the engines changed as the transport went to vertical flight. The floor began to roll and pitch gently, like the deck of a ship in a storm, as the transport started settling toward the ground, its two hundred tons balanced on the thrust of its lifters.

A new burst of sound came from aft, a hissing like a million snakes and a ripping noise like immense bedsheets being torn in half. The tail gunner was salvoing the pods of air-to-ground rockets, laying down a wall of explosions and flying metal and smoke between the transports and waiting enemy gunners. Blade scrambled into the front seat of his command jeep and tapped the driver on the shoulder. The man released the tie-downs and went through the correct motions for starting the engine, but Blade couldn't hear or feel a thing. The roar and vibration all around were too intense.

Suddenly there was a solid *thunk* from below as the landing gear hit the ground. Instantly the roar of the engines began to die as the pilots cut their throttles. Silence did not come. As the plane's engines faded, the motorcycles and vehicles began to roar and growl and belch smoke, and the tail gunner opened up with his twin 30mm cannon. Light poured in as the rear door swung open and down to the ground, forming a ramp. The first of the cycle troops were off the mark so fast they hit the end of the ramp before it hit the ground. They sailed off into the air, landing with thuds and squeals of tires. Somehow none of them were spilled into the path of their comrades. Four at a time, the rest of the cyclists thundered out after the first ones. For a moment Blade had the feeling of being caught up in a film about motorcycle gangs instead of a military operation. Then the deck ahead was clear. Without waiting for orders Blade's driver sent the jeep hurtling forward. It rolled down the deck, bounced wildly as it came off the ramp onto the ground, straightened out, and raced away from the transport.

Overhead the tail gunner was still firing random bursts.

As he ceased fire, Blade stood up in the jeep and looked around him. To the right and left the other transports were safely landed and pouring out their troops. Half a mile ahead lay the railroad yards, where organic raw material and food were brought in to build and feed the dragons and the matured dragons were taken out. Blade saw a train of the high-roofed dragon-carrying cars directly in his path. At the head, the locomotive was enveloped in the thick smoke of burning diesel fuel. Some of the cyclists were already working their way along the cars. Blade saw the flash of grenade and rocket explosions, doors flying off, and dying or wounded dragons lurching out to meet more grenades.

One dragon fell directly in the path of a cyclist who was moving too fast to stop. Man and machine flew high in the air, turning end over end. Blade's jeep bumped and rattled across the tracks of the railroad yard, leaving behind a rising pillar of smoke from the smashed and burning motorcycle.

The heavier armored cars and radio truck crossed the tracks faster and caught up with the jeep on the other side of the yard. The four vehicles rolled forward side by side.

A quick scan from left to right showed Blade four enemy-gun positions, none of them firing, all of them giving off thick clouds of smoke. In the nearest one the two guns pointed blackened and twisted barrels at the empty sky, while dismounted cyclists checked through the tents of the gunners to make sure that all the dead stayed that way. The rocket salvos had done good work.

The objective of Blade's Command Section was the base radio station. It was a substantial building, with two tall radio towers that would make good observation posts. Blade would set up his command post there. He didn't expect the strike force to need that much commanding, but it was always a good idea for the commanding officer to find a place where he could easily be found if necessary.

The jeep's radio remained silent as the Command Section rolled toward the station. No news was good news, in this case. Standard Operating Procedure for the raid called for radio silence from all units during the first fifteen minutes, unless something happened that called for a major change of plans.

They rolled past a long row of cylindrical concrete towers, like immense grain elevators. Those were the culture vats where the dragons were brought to viable size in tanks of nutrient fluid. From the top of one of them a machine gun sent bullets to kick up dust across the path of the Command Section. The turrets on the armored cars swiveled around, and two streams of tracer converged on the offending gun. The puffs of dust stopped abruptly. One of the cars swung out of line and fired a rocket at the base of the tower. It shivered, leaned almost elegantly to one side, shedding large slabs of concrete, then toppled in an explosion of dust. It cracked open as it fell, spewing out ruptured steel vats and piping, half-formed dragons, and a small lake of nutrient fluid. Blade ordered the car back in line. The culture vats were assigned to the demolition men of Company B. There was no point in wasting on them rockets that might be needed elsewhere.

The armored cars took the lead as the Command Section approached the radio station, with the radio truck behind them and the jeep in the rear. Three sections of motorcyclists moved into position on each flank to help clear the radio station and then form a headquarters reserve.

As the cyclists moved into position, two small helicopters skimmed in from the left, only a few feet above the ground. Both were armed, both were highly polished, and both carried Red Flame Security Administration markings. The machine gun in the door of the rear helicopter flickered, drawing another line of dust puffs across the ground toward the approaching vehicles. The radio truck lurched and started to skid as a tire blew. But the driver got it back under control, and all the vehicles in the strike force had wire-reinforced tires that could run deflated.

Both armored cars returned the fire of the helicopters. One of them dipped, struck the ground at full speed, and went cartwheeling along for a hundred yards, disintegrating into flaming pieces as it went. The other shivered, smoked, but kept on going and autorotated down out of sight behind the radio station.

The armored cars pulled up in front of the station door, training their guns on it and screening the radio truck and the jeep. The motorcyclists kept on, stopping and dismounting on either side of the building. A brief rattle of gunfire and smoke boiling up told Blade that they'd finished off the second helicopter.

Blade scrambled out of the jeep. The observation team climbed out the back of the radio truck and started toward one of the radio towers.

Suddenly a machine gun opened up from inside the radio station, followed by the sharp thumps of a grenade launcher. One grenade landed among the observation party, cutting down all four men. Blade threw himself flat on the ground as another grenade arched clear over the armored cars and exploded in his jeep. Fragments of the grenade, the jeep, and the driver showered down in all directions as the armored cars opened fire.

Blade saw windows and sections of wall disintegrate under the cars' point-blank machine-gun fire. Then two of the motorcyclists fired rockets through side windows. The blast blew off most of the roof from one end of the radio station and dropped the rest on top of the Russlanders inside. A wall of smoke boiled up from the wreckage. The dismounted motorcyclists moved toward it with fixed bayonets.

As they vanished into the smoke the radio finally came to life.

"Argus One to Nimrod. Argus One to Nimrod." That was a call from the commander of Company A, assaulting the garrison's barracks on the left flank.

"Nimrod to Argus One. Go ahead."

"We've got the ground opposition pretty thoroughly in hand. But there were six helicopters parked about a mile beyond the camp. One of them was an armed fire-support ship. It got our armored cars and mortar truck before we could get it. We're going to try getting a machine gun in range under cover of smoke."

"Acknowledged, Argus One. Execute. Nimrod out."

As Blade turned from the radio one of the cyclists ran out of the smoke. He was coughing and holding out a

Russland helmet in one hand. He stopped and saluted. "Sir, I thought you ought to see this."

Blade took the helmet. It was a standard Russland issue steel helmet, but freshly painted, varnished, waxed, and bearing the badge of the Fifth Guards Rifle Regiment. The Fifth Guards, Blade knew, was an elite Security unit. Its duties included providing troops for ceremonial occasions and bodyguards for traveling VIPs. From the amount of noise that was coming out of the radio station, it seemed the Fifth Guards also knew how to fight.

Blade was just about to call for reinforcements to help with the radio station when Argus One came back on the air.

"Nimrod, the other five helicopters have started their engines. They've also deployed a mortar platoon. Request permission to cancel moving the machine gun against the position without heavy-weapons support."

Blade decided to give it. There was no point in pushing a company across open ground into the teeth of mortar fire simply to pick off a few more helicopters. "Argus One, this is Nimrod. Permission—"

Blade was interrupted by a growing whistle from high above. Then the ground shivered as a salvo of mortar shells burst fifty yards from the radio station. In seconds, white smoke swallowed half an acre of ground.

"Argus One to Nimrod. The mortars have opened fire. We—"

"This is Nimrod. We know. I think we're the target." Another salvo, closer to the radio station, and more white smoke blotting out more of the landscape. "They appear to be laying down a smoke barrage around the radio station. Give me a mark when the helicopters take off, and also a direction."

"They're taking off now, leaving the mortars behind." A moment's silence. Then: "Nimrod, they seem to be headed your way, minimum altitude, slow speed."

"Thank you, Argus One."

As surely as if he'd overheard the enemy's orders, Blade knew what was happening here. Somewhere on the other side of the radio station was a Red Flame VIP and his bodyguards from Security's crack regiment. Over near Company A were the helicopters that had brought the man in. Now they were coming to try to bring him out, under cover of the smoke screen laid down by the mortars.

The Russlanders in the radio station would report all the enemy movements they could see. But the smoke that would screen the helicopters could also screen the armored cars. If he was willing to gamble—

Why not? One of the objectives of the raid was prisoners, and a Red Flame general would be a nice addition to the bag. Admittedly, this wasn't the sort of job a colonel should try to handle. He should delegate it to the man on the spot.

In this case, though, Colonel Richard Blade was the man on the spot.

He had no radio contact with the cyclists fighting inside the building. He could only hope they would keep their heads down, and that the Russlanders wouldn't use high-explosive mortar rounds so close to their own generals.

Quickly he briefed the armored car crews on his plan, then looked at his watch. The helicopters had about three miles to cover. That meant not more than five minutes' total traveling, and two minutes were already gone.

Blade climbed into the turret of the first car, watching the second hand clip away the seconds, listening to the endless thud of the smoke shells bursting on the far side of the radio station. He waited until he heard in the interval between two salvos the sound of the approaching helicopters. He raised his rifle in one hand and gave the signal.

Both drivers gunned their engines and the armored cars leaped forward. If Blade hadn't clamped one hand on the rim of the turret hatch, the sudden start would have thrown him clear. He crouched in the hatch as the cars roared around the building, squarely into what he hoped would be the path of the incoming helicopters. If there were five of them, they might outgun the cars. But the cars could take a great deal more punishment.

The first helicopter swept out of the murk so low that one landing skid nearly took off Blade's head. The gunner in the second car held his fire just long enough for the helicopter to pass over Blade, then fired. One burst did the job. At thirty yards the bullets must have gone right through the helicopter. The crash of its landing was lost in the roar of its exploding fuel. Blade ducked, knowing that a disintegrating rotor could lash about with enough force to slice a man in half.

His own car opened up on the second helicopter and he heard its engines die. But the third passed behind the second. As it came clear, its door gunner killed the second armored car's gunner with a well-placed burst. Then it landed, its rotors just clearing the shadowy wall of the radio station. Blade saw a door open in that wall and several running figures burst out. One of them wore a general officer's greatcoat and peaked hat and towered head and shoulders above the others. He must have been at least six feet eight.

The gunner of Blade's car opened up again at the helicopter. Blade saw the glass in the cockpit window shatter and the door gunner knocked backward into the cabin. He raised his rifle and sighted in on the running figures. He aimed low, wishing he had the marvelously precise Enfield 7. He wanted to disable, not kill. To have a prize like this snatched away by one misdirected bullet—

The running men went down, all of them still moving, still alive. Blade was changing magazines when he saw movement in the door of the helicopter. A dark egg shape flew out and rolled on the ground. Blade shot the man in the door, but the grenade had already rolled within reach of the tall general. He gripped it firmly, twisted the pin free, then heaved himself over to rest squarely on top of it. The explosion sounded just as the helicopter's fuel tanks gushed flame.

Blade sighed. General Golovin's habit of personally conducting key investigations had finally stretched his luck to the breaking point. It was unfortunate that he couldn't have been taken alive, but Blade could hardly blame Golovin for taking the same way out he himself might have used in similar circumstances.

In any case, Golovin was dead. A raid that cost the Red Flames their most brilliant counterespionage man could hardly be called unsuccessful, regardless of what else happened.

Quite a lot had happened while Blade was otherwise occupied, as he discovered when he was able to go back to commanding the strike force. While mopping up operations continued inside the radio station, Blade got on the command radio and took reports from each unit under his command.

The Demolition Group was in position. Three of the four tunnels from the dragon caves were blown, the fourth was rigged, and the main charges were ready for lowering into place at the dam. They'd had a little bit of trouble with two dozen dragons already on the surface ready for shipment, but that was over now.

The Blocking Group was also in position, and very bored. The two bridges were blown and there was no sign of an enemy within miles. Did they have permission to come up to join the fighting?

Permission denied. As much as Blade appreciated their kind of fighting spirit, he wasn't going to leave his back door unguarded. The Blocking Force would go on blocking.

It was harder to get a clear picture of the Battle Force. They'd struck hard and done their work thoroughly. In the process they'd become scattered all over the base, and were only just now regrouping to mop up and start collecting prisoners and wrecking facilities.

Casualties appeared to be light. One company had lost the better part of a platoon to an undetected gun position. Blade's own reserve had lost twelve men. Otherwise the casualty reports only trickled in by twos and threes.

Argus One came back on the air, reporting the overrunning of the mortar position. A few minutes later, Blade felt the ground start to shake at intervals as the Battle Group's demolition teams went to work. The thud of explosions came through the smoke, followed by the rumble and crashing of collapsing buildings and the crackle and roar of flames.

A captured enemy truck rolled past, two of the raiders in the cab and two more sitting in back. The rest of the back was filled with limp bodies in civilian clothes. The first load of prisoners was on its way back to the transports.

By now the smoke from the mortar barrage and the crashed helicopters was drifting away. Two demolitions men came up to Blade and asked for permission to set charges on the radio masts. Blade gave the permission, scrambled up on top of the radio truck, and sat on the roof.

Now the attack planes came roaring in low overhead, ten of them. Blade tuned in on their frequency, listening to their cheerful comments on the shambles unfolding below. After a minute he got their report.

Their job was also done. Two planes had gone down over the target, but the only first-class enemy airfield within five hundred miles would be out of action for at least a couple of days. They'd shot down five enemy fighters over the field, and on the way here they'd added four light-attack planes, a transport, and two helicopters to the score.

Blade gave them a "Well Done," but he couldn't give them any targets. The dragon base was disintegrating so rapidly under the hands of the strike force that there was nothing left for the pilots to do except fly air cover until the job was done.

Blade signaled to the driver of the radio truck, and it headed for the pilots' planned drop zone near the canyon of the dragon caves. Rounding up the pilots was something Blade wanted to supervise himself. Everything else seemed to be well under control.

The biggest explosion yet shook the ground so violently that the driver nearly lost control of the truck. For a moment Blade wondered if the Demolition Group had blown the dam prematurely. Then he saw flames and smoke mounting toward the sky from the fuel dump. The smoke rose to join the vast cloud that already hung over the base, casting its shadow on the ruins. The only thing that seemed to be intact anywhere on the landscape was one of the breeding vats. As Blade watched, smoke puffed up from its base and it split apart. Most of it fell to the ground and the rest stuck up like a solitary jagged tooth.

The roar of assault transports lifting off sounded overhead. Blade looked up to see the transports of the Demolition Group pass, shifting as he watched from vertical to horizontal flight. That meant the charges on the dam were set and fused. Blade checked the left breast pocket of his battledress. On a slip of paper, there was the code to detonate the fuses by radio command if the timers didn't work.

As Blade's truck rolled into the drop area the pilots started abandoning their planes. One by one they swung low and slow over the area, pulled up, and ejected. The ejection seats kicked them up and clear, then their white and yellow parachutes streamed out behind them and they began drfiting down all over the area. The cyclists roared off to pick them up. Blade sensed an urgency in their speed, a desire to get the job done and follow the Demolition Group out of here!

Blade's truck pulled up at the very edge of the canyon. As he climbed out, the transport of the Blocking Group roared overhead, its wings swinging back to the high-speed position. Its engines flamed brightly as the pilot cut in the afterburners in his eagerness to get away.

One by one the pilotless attack planes plunged to the ground and exploded. Blade saw one strike the edge of the canyon, bounce, and tumble down onto the dragons far below. Blade watched as the monsters charged about in mounting panic, trampling and attacking one another, battering themselves against the rock, trying vainly to climb the canyon walls.

The pilot of the last plane nearly followed it into the canyon. Blade saw him drifting down toward the edge, shouted at him, but knew that his words were lost in the roars of the dragons.

At the last moment the pilot spilled air from his parachute. It collapsed, dropping him twenty feet to the ground. He landed no more than inches from the edge. Blade and two other men sprinted to grab the pilot before his chute dragged him into the canyon. They caught him with no more than seconds to spare. As Blade knelt, with both hands clamped on one of the pilot's boots, he saw the lake behind the dam heave up into a monstrous white dome of water.

All three charges must have gone off together. The damn did not crumble, it was blown away by the combined force of the explosions and the water they drove before them. A section of dam three hundred feet wide and two hundred feet high was gone before the shock or sound of the explosion reached Blade. Then the roar of the water followed, and after that the roar of the dragons.

Blade forced himself to watch as the flood thundered down the canyon, a wall of water a hundred feet high. It tossed live dragons, dead dragons, boulders the size of a house like chips of wood. It swept along at a mile a minute, throwing up a curtain of spray so thick it seemed the canyon was filling with smoke. By the time the flood passed below where Blade was standing, the spray rose halfway to the canyon's edge. It was thick enough to blot out the view of what was happening below, but the roar of the water was not loud enough to drown out the dying roars of the dragons.

If the dragons had been natural creatures, however dangerous, Blade could have taken no pleasure in such wholesale slaughter. But their origins were unnatural, so there was nothing he could regret in the way they'd died.

He led the others away from the canyon's rim until the roar of the water began to fade. Then he stopped and said to everyone within earshot:

"Well done, gentlemen. Now—let's go home."

Chapter 24

All eleven of the assault transports got home. So did all but fifty of the men of Strike Force Blade. They brought with them more than a hundred prisoners, plus a mixed but valuable loot of files, code books, instruments, and so on.

Behind them they left nearly a thousand enemies dead and a mission thoroughly accomplished. They had smashed the ability of the Red Flames to wage genetic warfare, and they'd done a good deal more besides.

General Golovin's death would throw Red Flame counterespionage into confusion, and the inevitable purge of his followers would throw it into chaos. It would take at least a year for Red Flame counterespionage to recover, the most crucial year of the war.

The debut of the assault transports had even more spectacular effects. Within two weeks after the raid, the Red Flames withdrew from their armies on the Gallic frontier no less than ten divisions, with all their supporting troops and air cover. They were assigned to home defense. Meanwhile, the Empire of Englor was able to reinforce the Eighth Army with five infantry divisions and the Seventy-first Airmobile Brigade. The Red Flame offensive into Gallia was certainly off, at least until the following spring. By that time the Eighth Army would be strong enough not only to defend itself but also to destroy its enemies.

R summed things up:

"Never before in the history of human conflict have so few thrown so many into so great a panic in so little time."

So it was not surprising that Strike Force Blade was made a standing unit. It was renamed Number Twelve Commando and placed permanently under the control of the Special Operations Division.

It was not surprising that General Sir Morgan Strong was placed on the retired list. There were some who wanted to try him by court-martial, but it was generally felt that he would be punished enough by having to spend the rest of the war raising chickens in Dorsetshire.

Finally, it was not surprising that Colonel Richard Blade received from the hand of His Imperial Majesty Charles VI Englor's highest military decoration, the Imperial Cross.

"Every man of your strike force seems to have performed some deed worthy of this award," said the Emperor as he pinned the Cross on Blade's tunic. "But naturally, we cannot contrive to award six hundred Imperial Crosses. So we present this award not only for your own exceptional and heroic services, but in recognition of those of every man under your command."

"I understand, Sire," said Blade.

It was a gray day in London, and the first snow that seemed likely to stay on the ground was falling slowly. R was already seated in the back of the Rolls-Royce as Blade and Rilla came out arm-in-arm to join him.

This time they were not going away on a vacation. In Blade's attaché case was the complete material on the assault transports, including the formulas for the alloys and the chemical fuel. He was going north to the Midlands to discuss improved designs for the transports with Avro's engineers.

In Rilla's case lay her complete notes on genetic manipulation and cloning processes. She was going still farther north, to the University of Edinburgh. There she would be talking about her discoveries with several leading doctors and biologists. She would not be talking about their military potential, but about their value against cancer. Blade could sense the enormous happiness this brought her. He could almost see her glowing in the dirty twilight that was settling down over London.

The twilight settled down even faster as they drove out toward the airport. Blade leaned back in his seat, held Rilla's hand, and stared at the two cleared semicircles made by the windshield wipers.

"Tired, Richard?" said R. For once his voice sounded exactly like J's.

Blade smiled. "Not tired, exactly. A little beaten down, perhaps, by all the Court activities. I'll take great care never to win another high award, if I can manage it. I can cope with the Russlanders, but the Imperial Court's another matter."

R laughed. "I doubt if you're going to be able to manage that. Not as long as you're commanding Special Operations Division's private army, and I assure you it will be some time before you can lay down that job."

"Perhaps," said Rilla quietly. For a moment her smile

seemed a trifle forced. She accepted the possibility of Blade's being killed, but it was not precisely her favorite topic of conversation.

Blade squeezed Rilla's hand and reached into his coat pocket for his cigarettes. His hand was just closing on the pack when black night and red fire seemed to explode in his head.

He heard himself groan, he felt his hand clamping tightly on Rilla's, and he heard her gasp with the pain of his grip. He knew what was happening to him. Lord Leighton's computer was seizing control of his brain, twisting it so that once more he would live and move in Home Dimension, in England instead of Englor.

What should he do about Rilla? If he held onto her, she might come with him, files, discoveries, knowledge, everything. But if she came with him, would she survive the journey across the Dimensions to Englor? Could she—?

Then he realized that he now had no choice, because the pain in his head had frozen all his muscles so that he couldn't have released Rilla's hand if he'd wanted to. The pain pounded and swelled in his head, coming in great waves, the waves slowly blending into one continuous roar.

Yet he could still think clearly, and the thought that now filled his mind was almost as nightmarish as the dragons. R was sitting there in the seat beside him, watching everything that was happening, that would happen. R was watching—through the haze of pain Blade could still make out the man's face, a face showing intense concentration and burning curiosity. R was watching, and he would go on watching until the seat beside him was empty.

Perhaps R had not discovered the secret of Blade's origins before. But now—now he would have in his hands nearly all he needed to guess it, to guess the secret of Dimension X.

Then, mercifully, the pain blanked out the last of Blade's ability to think about anything.

Chapter 25

Blade sat down in the brown leather armchair facing the fire, and J sat down in the black leather one.

"Whiskey?" said J.

Blade shook his head. He wanted to wrap up the debriefing and go home. He was both mentally and physically exhausted in a way he'd seldom been in his life.

"Very well," said the older man. He lit a cigar and puffed in silence for a few moments.

"The alloys and the fuel you brought back go hand in hand," he said finally. "The planes built with the alloys need the fuel to get maximum performance. And of course the planes using the fuel have to be built with the alloys. Otherwise their engines will simply melt."

"I suspected as much," said Blade. "What are the prospects for producing either?"

"Good enough so that the production rights will probably be worth an immediate million pounds," said J. "If there was a prospect of bringing either or both into production at once, we'd ask ten million. But anyone who buys the rights will have to spend several years and several million pounds of their own money duplicating certain catalysts and setting up production facilities. The picture is quite promising, however."

Blade found that he could not pay as much attention to promising pictures as he ought to. Admittedly, once the fuel and alloys were perfected, Britain's aerospace industry would lead the world. But that was for the future. There were more urgent matters on his mind.

"What about Rilla?"

"Her notes are exceptionally complete, by the standards of her own Dimension. However, much of what was common knowledge there isn't quite so common here. Again, we have something whose value is enormous and can be realized fairly easily. It won't be another case like teksin. But it will be a few years before we can use Miss Haran's discoveries, either for curing cancer or for building dragons."

The attempted humor fell flat. Blade sensed that J's heart was not in it in any case.

"No, I meant—how is Rilla herself? I haven't been let in to see her, so I assume she's still recovering from the transition, but—"

"Richard," said J quietly, and the soft voice held enormous compassion for the younger man. "Rilla has quite recovered, physically. But mentally—she is not doing too well."

"How—badly?" said Blade.

"She has no more mind than a six-month-old baby," said J.

There was a long silence. Blade stared into the fire. He had seldom felt worse in all his life in *any* Dimension. Rilla's mind was gone, and when all was said and done, it was his fault. He *could* have left her in Englor.

"Thank you," he said, and rose to go.

Richard Blade walked along Westminster Embankment. Above him the sky was gray, and from it fell the same kind of snow that had been falling on the London of Englor when he left it. His mood was as bleak and as gray as the weather.

He had done his duty to England and to Englor, and even more effectively than usual. He'd helped alter the course of history in Englor's Dimension, and what he'd brought back might yet do the same here.

Yet, didn't he also have duties to people like Rilla? Wasn't there perhaps a point where they took over? Genetics or no genetics, he would not have been betraying his own country by not bringing Rilla home. The alloys and the fuel would have been worth the trip. Rilla could still be safe and sane, honored and prosperous in Englor instead of helpless in a hospital in England.

He looked up at the tower of Big Ben, looming through the falling snow. No dragons of the Red Flames would perch there again in Englor; none would ever do so here in England.

That was a victory. But was it worth it, when other people so often seemed to pay the price?

Blade didn't know. Perhaps there was no answer. In any case, he would have to go on doing his duty, whether or not he ever found the answer.